on track ...
Jethro Tull

every album, every song

Jordan Blum

Sonicbond Publishing Limited
www.sonicbondpublishing.co.uk
Email: info@sonicbondpublishing.co.uk

First Published in the United Kingdom 2019
First Published in the United States 2019

Reprinted 2020

British Library Cataloguing in Publication Data:
A Catalogue record for this book is available from the British Library

Copyright Jordan Blum 2019

ISBN 978-1-78952-016-3

Typeset in ITC Garamond & Berthold Akzidenz Grotesk
Printed and bound in England

Graphic design and typesetting: Full Moon Media

on track ...
Jethro Tull

every album, every song

Jordan Blum

SONIC**BOND**
PUBLISHING

sonicbondpublishing.co.uk

Acknowledgements

First, I would like to thank Stephen Lambe for offering me the opportunity to write this book and for showing nonstop confidence in my ability to produce something accurate, interesting, enlightening and generally worthwhile. Similarly, thanks to fellow Sonicbond Publishing writer – and my Classic Rock Society editor – Steve Pilkington for his support and advice along the way, as well as to Tim Bowness, currently giving Sonicbond books a home at the Burning Shed online store.

In terms of personal contributions, author Brian Rabey deserves gratitude for his insights and friendship as this book came together. Likewise, thanks to all of the musicians who answered my questions about their histories with Jethro Tull; whether or not your responses are explicitly referenced, know that your feedback was invaluable in helping me shape my research as I went. (These musicians include Colin Edwin, Fred Schendel, Ian Beabout, James Schoen, Karl Eisenhart, Mark Trueack, Mathew Spivack, Mike Keneally, Mike Toehinder, Neal Morse, Petter Sandström, Phideaux Xavier, Randy George, Rikard Sjöblom, Ross Jennings, Steve Hackett, and Tim Bowness). Equal thanks to everyone who submitted pieces for the photo section: Austin Kokel, Bob Keith, Bruce Kessler, Claus Petersen, Guido Verbiest, James Griffiths, John Goldacker, Michael Gillett, Philipp Rauch, and Thomas Friesenhagen.

Finally, thanks to all of my friends, family, and online acquaintances whose constant interest in and advice for this project made me believe in and stay focused on what I was doing. Specifically, thank you to my sister, Erica, and my mother, Kandie, for their love and support in everything I do. Most importantly, thank you to my father, Jay, for not only being there as a parent but also for introducing me to progressive music when I was a kid. The origin of this book – as well as everything I am as a genre fan and writer – dates back to you playing me those albums in the basement when I was young. I guess blasting *Thick as a Brick* and *A Passion Play* almost every day during high school paid off.

on track ...
Jethro Tull

Contents

Introduction

It's nearly impossible to discuss the history of rock music without praising the monumental quality, impact, variety, and boldness of Britain's Jethro Tull. Named after an eighteenth-century agriculturalist – and not after their striking frontman, despite the common claim of both casual listeners and uninitiated spectators – the group almost immediately became one of the most ambitious, and significant acts in two simultaneous subsections of the genre: progressive rock and folk rock (thus, we subsequently have the term 'progressive folk'). Alongside English contemporaries like Genesis, King Crimson, Pink Floyd, Van Der Graaf Generator, Gentle Giant, Yes, Camel, and Renaissance, Jethro Tull helped invent not only new sights and sounds within burgeoning forms (including innovative integrations of already established styles), but also freshly experimental techniques *within* those encompassing evolutions ('epic' song lengths, conceptual sequences, elaborate meta-packings, and more). Naturally, they also managed to become a staple of stadium/arena rock as well; as such, they were among the most financially successful and popular bands of the 1970s, leading to tenure on classic rock radio stations across the globe to this very day. In other words, Jethro Tull have always been, and will always be, kind of a big deal.

Officially formed in 1967 (following a few years of fledgeling roadblocks, such as different monikers and line-up changes that contained some players who would return later), mastermind Ian Anderson and company initially (i.e., 1967's debut LP, *This Was*) encompassed a palpable blues and jazz foundation. They before subsequently veered towards more sophisticated, diverse, and expansive – though still warm and charming – elements (including a strong vocal shift for Anderson, which we'll get to soon enough). Next, their early '70s period – which, let's be honest, is often considered their peak –was ripe with lasting progressive rock benchmarks in the form of iconic album cuts ('Aqualung', 'Bungle in the Jungle') and lengthy narrative suites both sardonically endearing (*Thick as a Brick*) and segregationally erudite (*A Passion Play*).

For the most part, the band spent the latter half of that decade modulating those trademark flavours, ultimately finishing the '70s with what they referred to as the 'folk rock trilogy' (*Songs from the Wood*, *Heavy Horses*, and *Stormwatch*). Like numerous peers at the time (ELP, Rush, Yes, and King Crimson, to varying degrees), Jethro Tull then embraced the more commercially accessible arrangement and songwriting demands that most of the 1980s popular culture wrought – complete with a fair share of electronic percussion, six-stringed hard rock fervour, and synthy highlights – yet their core identity remained throughout.

As their output came to a close in the '90s, the group more or less adapted that streamlined slant for the norms and expectations of the time; ironically, however, Jethro Tull concurrently recalled the cosier and more robust and go-getting assets of their mid to late '70s triumphs. This compromise even extended into Anderson's 2012 solo sequel, *Thick as a Brick 2: Whatever Happened to Gerald Bostock?*. In a way, then, they nearly came full circle at the end, leaving behind a remarkably cherished, consistent, and commanding discography.

Retrospectively, such a trajectory makes Jethro Tull not only one of the premiere progressive rock artists of all time, but arguably the single most influential progressive folk ensemble ever (not to undervalue the significance of stylistic siblings like Fairport Convention, The Strawbs, Steeleye Span, and Pentangle, of course). Specifically, Jethro Tull's fingerprints can be found on the works of various modern acts, including – but far from limited to – Porcupine Tree, Dream Theater, Änglagård, Opeth, Midlake, Big Big Train, Fleet Foxes, Of Monsters and Men, Joanna Newsom, The Decemberists, Agalloch, and Phideaux.

Several notable creators have been sweetly forthright in extolling Jethro Tull's bearing on themselves and the genres above in general. In particular, guitarist Steve Hackett (ex-Genesis) reflects, 'They elevated folk rock to electric proportions and sounded more disciplined than many of the bands of the early era. They've always ploughed their own furrow with wide dynamics, which work particularly well live. Ian's fantastic voice, flute-playing, and sense of perfectionism – along with Martin Barre's marvellous guitar work – was always a treat for me'.

Clearly, there's a lot to dissect about the group's studio legacy, which is exactly what this book aims to do. Going album by album, we'll look at the behind-the-scenes circumstances and motivations for each release before delving into a track-by-track original analysis (with periodic input from outside players and professionals along the way) to acutely observe why Jethro Tull was – and always will be – an invaluable part of rock music history.

This Was (1968)

Personnel:
Mick Abrahams: guitars (six and nine string), backing and lead vocals (4)
Ian Anderson: lead vocals (1 – 3, 7, and 9), flute, piano, guitar, harmonica, clanghorn
Clive Bunker: drums, hooter, charm bracelet
Glenn Cornick: bass guitar
Dee Palmer: French horn and orchestral arrangements (4)
Victor Gamm: engineer
Produced at Sound Techniques, London, June – August 1968 by Jethro Tull and Terry Ellis
UK release date: October 1968. US release date: February 1969.
Highest chart places: UK: 10, USA: 62
Running time: 38:21
Current edition: Rhino 2018 three-CD/one-DVD '50th Anniversary' Edition (Steven Wilson Remixed)

In his book *Mountains Come Out of the Sky: The Illustrated History of Prog Rock*, Will Romano notes: 'Historically, progressive rock had been forged from the musical fires lit by American blues and R&B pioneers'. Arguably no other early entry in a genre better exemplifies this than Jethro Tull's premiere outing, 1968's *This Was*. Filled with stimuli from across the Atlantic (a trend that had been occurring in England since before the British Invasion sparked reciprocal emulation in America), the LP was borne out of a handful of roster and name changes over the preceding three years. Yet it still carried the stylistic identity that schoolmates Ian Anderson, Jeffrey Hammond, and John Evan aimed for years before Jethro Tull formally began. Hence, *This Was*, like the first collections by several peers (Genesis' *From Genesis to Revelation*, Pink Floyd's *The Piper at the Gates of Dawn*, and Yes' eponymous work, for instance), alluded to the band's future DNA while also standing in stark contrast from it. In addition, it's a fine example of how (as the saying goes) greatness comes from humble beginnings.

Internally, the most notable aspect of it is easily the weight of Mick Abrahams (who only appeared on this one and would then go on to form Blodwyn Pig). As a co-writer on several tracks and the lead vocalist on one ('Move on Alone'), Abrahams' role makes *This Was* a surprisingly communal endeavour in hindsight (since he departed because Anderson wanted to go in a different direction and take on a more dominant role afterwards). Even the liner notes included a telling anecdote – 'This was how we were playing then – but things change – don't they?' – that was echoed by Anderson in a March 2018 remembrance for *PROG* magazine:

> *It's all in the title, isn't it? This was Jethro Tull. That's no accident because when we were recording it, the one thing I felt sure about is that if we*

were lucky enough to make another album, I knew it wouldn't be like this one: based on blues elements and black American folk culture. That's not part of my life and I couldn't keep doing that – I'd look like a complete twit.

It's also worth noting how much *This Was* showed a reliance on instrumentals (four) and, like early Beatles LPs, reimagined material from other musicians ('Serenade to a Cuckoo' and 'Cat's Squirrel' originated with Roland Kirk and Isaiah 'Doctor' Ross, respectively). Likewise, it finds Anderson alternating between his more recognisable vocal timbre and a lower bellow – which he'd completely abandon soon after – that overtly evoked his overseas R&B counterparts.

Upon release, *This Was* sold well, was received favourably by outlets like *Melody Maker* and *New Musical Express* and charted highly in the UK (it was met positively but less enthusiastically overall in the US). Looking back, it's obvious that it contained several key components of the group's trademark sound, such as feisty drumming, biting six-string licks, and flowery flute passages (which are particularly impressive considering that Anderson had only taken up the instrument about six weeks prior to recording). It's no surprise, then, that devotees see it as a vital, if occasionally overlooked, part of the Jethro Tull chronology.

'My Sunday Feeling' (Anderson)
With its initial burst of shuffling beats, focused bass lines, tight guitar chords, interspersed flute flourishes, and tenderly penitent vocals, this opening track immediately reveals how much Jethro Tull was touched by the blues back then. Even its lyrics – 'Now that the night is over / Got to clear my head so I can see / Till I get to put together / That old feeling won't let me be' – are emblematically simple, blunt, and regretful. While everyone plays their part efficiently (and the mid-section duel between Abrahams and Anderson is alluring and ambitious), it's Bunker who shines most, as he proves ceaselessly dynamic and creative in leading the charge. It's also worth noting that the closing portion subtly conjures to 'Work Song' (by Nat Adderley and Oscar Brown) and 'Pink Panther Theme' (by Henry Mancini).

'Some Day the Sun Won't Shine for You' (Anderson)
A slower and sparser tune than its predecessor, this one evokes 'Key to the Highway' by Big Bill Broonzy in both its overtly traditional structure and instrumentation (including some impressive harmonica fills). Light and mellow, it finds Anderson and Abrahams sharing lead vocals with a definite shade of DIY appeal (since their phrasing wasn't consistently synchronised). The absence of Bunker and Cornick makes it an atypical inclusion, too, and there's an inherently bittersweet nature to how well the other pair match each other vocally and instrumentally when one considers the behind-the-

scenes turmoil and subsequent split between them.

'Beggar's Farm' (Abrahams, Anderson)

Without a doubt, 'Beggar's Farm' is the most prophetic track on *This Was*. Just about every element – from the woodwind warnings and revolving guitar patterns to the cautionary singing and purposefully stifled percussion – hints at the sinister air of upcoming gems like 'Sweet Dream' and multiple cuts from 1971's *Aqualung*. It's also the first time on the record that Anderson sings in what would become his recognised register; equally, the relatively erratic complexity near the end, while planted a bit in freeform jazz, also suggests aspects of later work (as do Anderson's respiratory alarms, however compulsory). In a June 2018 interview with *Rolling Stone* magazine, he called the song, 'a relatively successful attempt to take the essence of black American blues and turn it into some middle-class white boy [music]'; in the process, though, the band foreshadowed the great pieces they'd soon devise.

'Move on Alone' (Abrahams)

The only selection written and sung solely by Abrahams on the album (and therefore, on any of their studio LPs), 'Move on Alone' is a strikingly different composition than its brethren. In fact, the mixture of Abrahams' nostalgic and classy delivery, coupled with Dee (formerly David) Palmer's horn arrangement, makes it sound more like, say, a lost track from Love's *Forever Changes* or The Moody Blues' *Days of Future Past* (or even the big band creations of decades past) than it does an expected continuation of the established *This Was* path. Similarly, the ways in which the bright and bouncy score contrasts the downtrodden foundation and melancholic views – 'My bed is so empty and my heart is grown cold /Guess I'll just die before I grow old' – is admirable. It's precisely that diversity that makes it such a treasured addition and demonstrates how determined Jethro Tull were from the start.

'Serenade to a Cuckoo' (Roland Kirk)

Roland Kirk was a major force in the 1960s avant-garde jazz movement, as well as a major reason for why Anderson brought flute into the quartet's sound (in addition to him not wanting to be yet another 'third-rate guitarist'). Thus, their rendition of this introductory tune from Kirk's 1964 album, *I Talk with the Spirits*, is both an explicitly engaging centrepiece and an intrinsically loving nod to a prevailing influence. A tad longer than the original, this one forgoes the piano backing for a warmer, livelier, and more straightforward take that lulls you in and never lets go.

'Dharma for One' (Anderson, Bunker)

As one of only two pieces co-written by Bunker on *This Was*, 'Dharma for One' logically radiates unrestrained percussion that, when combined with

13

the surrounding textural frenzy, actually foreshadows a specific breakdown
in 1972's *Thick as a Brick*. (It also features the claghorn, an instrument that
both Anderson and eventual bassist Jeffrey Hammond claim to have invented).
Before that, however, the opening section is fairly accessible and effective,
with some truly beautiful melodic lines. Likely the most famous and beloved
entry on the album, it certainly ranks as its best instrumental, resulting in it
becoming a staple of early concerts (with added words and more intensity on
occasion, oddly enough). Several other artists also covered it in the ensuing
couple years alone, such as Pesky Gee, The Ides of March, and Ekseption.

'It's Breaking Me Up' (Anderson)
Another traditional blues track (with lovelorn outcries like 'Ah, baby, I said
you're breaking me up woman / You're breaking me down / Your lovely little
pieces / Scattered all around'), this one sets itself apart with its waltz time,
fervent guitar and harmonica juxtapositions, and subtly gruff singing (another
trademark Anderson would develop more over time). Although they stick to a
conventional and basic plan, Bunker and Cornick still warrant nods here for
keeping the momentum invigorating and focused; likewise, Abrahams plays
it safe as well yet inarguably channels the styles of other prodigious blues
guitarists like Eric Clapton and B.B. King. All in all, a satisfying standard.

'Cat's Squirrel' (Isaiah Ross, Abrahams)
The penultimate instrumental on *This Was*, 'Cat's Squirrel', like 'Serenade to
a Cuckoo', is an adaption of someone else's song (in this case, Doctor Ross
and the Orbits' 1961classic). Its lack of words is an obvious difference between
the two, and its most striking feature is the three-way power that Abrahams,
Bunker, and Cornick emit, with the latter duo providing a bustling foundation
on which the former's piercing outcries lie. It's also interesting that Jethro
Tull chose not to include any harmonica (since the original has so much), plus
how empty the middle portion is compared to the consistent density of Ross'
version. As such, it's a less faithful interpretation than even Cream's two years
prior, but it nevertheless compels in its own way and serves as a fine example
of how groups in the late '60s had a penchant for fruitfully stretching out their
covers.

'A Song for Jeffrey' (Anderson)
'A Song for Jeffrey' is significant for a few reasons. Aside from being one of the
more popular and enduring songs from the record, it was also the only single
to also appear on it. In addition, it kicked off a pattern of dedicating one track
per album to Hammond that would continue on *This Was*' two immediate
successors, 1969's *Stand Up* and 1970's *Benefit*. Lines like 'Gonna lose my
way tomorrow / Gonna give away my car', joined with the chorus, support
that explanation that the track portrays Hammond 'in slightly condescending
terms as someone with emotional problems who lost his way easily'. As for its

music, Anderson's chilling flute passages and Abrahams' slide guitar are clear highlights, and Anderson's deep blues pastiche is at its most tangible here, for sure. The quartet's ability to seamlessly balance light and heavy amalgamations is also a joy.

'Round' (Bunker, Cornick, Anderson, Abrahams, Ellis)

The only track credited to the entire quartet (and producer Terry Ellis), it closes the debut with a minute-long slice of peaceful piano motifs with light accompaniments. Interestingly, all of that fades away toward the second half, allowing Anderson's lone woodwind outro to leave listeners in idyllic splendour. It works well as a modest coda that once again signifies the role jazz played in Jethro Tull at the time.

Bonuses and contemporary tracks

'Sunshine Day' (Abrahams)

The first single from the *This Was* era (released in early 1968, alongside B-side 'Aeroplane'), 'Sunshine Day' is immediately engrossing because of how well Abrahams' backing vocals blend with Anderson's forefront singing to produce amazingly luminous harmonies. Of course, Cornick and Bunker light blue rhythms scuffle along jubilantly as well, as do Abrahams' crunchy riffs (especially during the instrumental change-up halfway through). All in all, 'Sunshine Day' surely made a strong impression on countless first-time listeners.

'Love Story' (Anderson)

Appropriately put out with 'Christmas Song' in December 1968, this one instantly impresses with its dynamic back-and-forth outline between soft drum, flute and electric guitar contemplations and several full-bodied reflections. Aside from Abrahams' marginally psychedelic timbre, the standout detail is Anderson's phrasing and timbre, both of which foreshadow his presence on the subsequent *Stand Up* and *Benefit*. It's odd that the first Jethro Tull outing is the latest to be remixed by Steven Wilson (Porcupine Tree, no-man). As always, he did a bang-up job with it, offering a mono original, stereo remix, 4.1 DTS, and 5.1 surround versions of *This Was* and associated recordings (alternate versions of album cuts, plus 'Love Story', 'Christmas Song', and 'Ultimate Confusion'), in addition to the 1968 Live BBC sessions and a couple of US FM radio spots. It's a superb handling of the sequence that started it all.

Stand Up (1969)

Personnel:

Ian Anderson: vocals, flute, mandolin, acoustic guitar, Hammond organ, piano, mouth organ, balalaika

Martin Barre: electric guitar, flute (2, 9)

Clive Bunker: drums, percussion

Glenn Cornick: bass guitar (except for 5)

Andy Johns: engineer, bass guitar (5)

Dee Palmer: string arrangements and conductor (9)

James Grashow: cover art

Produced at Morgan Studios, London (except 'Bourée', which was produced at Olympic Sound Studio 1), April – May 1969 by Ian Anderson and Terry Ellis

UK release date: July 1969. US release date: September 1969.

Highest chart places: UK: 1, USA: 20

Running time: 37:48

Current edition: Rhino 2016 two-CD/one DVD 'Elevated Edition' (Steven Wilson Remixed)

As impressive as *This Was*, well, was at the time, it also struggled a bit from an identity crisis and a lack of developed and confident freshness. Put another way, its reliance on repeating established devices and using outside inputs prevented the LP from fully launching Jethro Tull as its own distinctive creative force. Fortunately, that problem was solved mere months later, with *Stand Up*. Rather than suffer the dreaded 'sophomore slump', its advancements in songwriting, variety, musicianship, and general innovation showcased a 'coming of age' and 'pivotal' (as Anderson puts it) accumulation that's superior in every way.

Of course, the catalyst for *Stand Up*'s progression came during and immediately after *This Was*, with Anderson and Abrahams – who saw himself as a co-leader at the time – butting heads over where the group should go next. In the aftermath, Abrahams left, and Anderson became the proper mastermind behind Jethro Tull, leaving himself free to steer their sound into a more classical and folk rock direction. Likewise, its focus on Anderson's relationship with his parents (in addition to him wrestling with his recent celebrity) signalled a desire for conceptual exploration that would later dominate some of Jethro Tull's most revered releases.

The impact of Abraham's replacement, Martin Barre, can't be understated, either. Initially competing 'nervous[ly]' against several other musicians for the job (including ex-The Nice guitarist David O'List, Stealers Wheel bassist Tony Williams, John Mayall Bluesbreakers' guitarist Mick Taylor and Black Sabbath guitarist Tony Iommi (who appeared with Jethro Tull in 1968's *The Rolling Stones Rock and Roll Circus*), he brought a markedly more skilled and multifaceted approach than his predecessor. As a result – and because he appeared on every subsequent record, too – his style instantly came to define the Jethro Tull sound about as much as any of Anderson's contributions. In regard to this initial outing with the remaining trio (and his first appearance on any album), Barre found *Stand Up* quite thrilling, to say the least.

Considering that the front of *This Was* made many people believe that the group consisted of old men, it's no surprise that, as Anderson recollects in Brian Rabey's book *A Passion Play*, they 'began working on the cover ... before [they] even began recording'. Specifically, producer Terry Ellis had a wood cutting artist named James Grashow meet with them during a show in New Haven, Connecticut in February 1969. (Reportedly, he continued to work with them for about a week to better capture them.) In keeping with the LP's title, the original vinyl release opened like a children's pop-up book, revealing a cut-out of the band (leading to *Stand Up* winning the *New Musical Express* award for best album artwork of the year). Although subsequent reissues dropped that gimmick, it remains an iconic image.

Critically, it fared far better in both the UK and the US, achieving top chart placements and a greater number of positive reviews. Over the years, many admirers – plus Anderson himself – have praised it as a favourite effort. It's not hard to hear why, either, as the quartet's quick development was a remarkable feat by any measure.

'A New Day Yesterday' (Anderson)
Intentionally or not, this piece (which was the first recorded for *Stand Up*) acts as the perfect bridge between the first and second collections, as nearly every part of its raucous blues edge makes it feel like a carryover from *This Was*. Even so, there are already signs of a heavier and more challenging vision, especially in Barre's playing. For the most part, he stabilises Bunker and Cornick's flow with unassuming chords and riffs, yet his tone is noticeably sharper than Abrahams'. Honestly, though, it's his brief solo roughly halfway through that truly makes his unique presence felt. It's here that he exposes not only what he'll bring to the Jethro Tull formula from then onward, but also how the growing genre of heavy metal may have faintly influenced their direction. Anderson's daunting flute and harmonica breaks are also telling treats.

'Jeffrey Goes to Leicester Square' (Anderson)
The second of the Jeffrey Hammond-based trilogy spread across Jethro Tull's first three outings, 'Jeffrey Goes to Leicester Square' is where the quartet's change in direction rightly commences. Playful and vibrant from the start, its light blend of balalaika strums, bass taps, high-pitched bells, woodwinds, and Far East percussion signifies the more startling and eclectic style of *Stand Up*. Similarly, Anderson's engaging melody and endearing omniscient narrative – 'Bright city woman / Where did you learn all the things you say? / You listen to the newsmen on TV / You may fool yourself, but you don't fool me' – pinpoint the commanding quality he'd soon be known for.

To this day, Anderson credits it with helping Stand Up find prodigious success in the UK, noting that its 'sort [of] quirky, English feel' made it 'one of those more original and unusual pieces that ... caught the fancy of British fans'. Indeed, it's arguably the first song in their arsenal to accurately nail what made them so special.

'Bourée' (J.S. Bach, arrangement by Anderson)

A 'cocktail jazz' version (as Anderson reflects) of Bach's celebrated selection, 'Bourée' is both the only cover and the only instrumental on the LP (which intrinsically validates Jethro Tull's improvement as an artistic force. Fortunately, it does an excellent job of infusing Bach's template with myriad layers of treasured Jethro Tull trademarks, like Anderson's flamboyant flute wails, Bunker's syncopated tricks, and Cornick's ceaselessly inventive and fetching movements. On the whole, it's a breezier, denser, and more fleshed-out reimagining that exemplifies their enhancements as musicians and composers. Considering that, as Cornick reminisces, it arose out of 'the most disastrous recording session [he] ever did' and was only completed after Anderson 'edited the song together from bits and pieces and then added some extra stuff', the fact that it works so well is particularly praiseworthy.

'Back to the Family' (Anderson)

As its title proposes, this entry finds Anderson wishing for a respite from the stresses of the music industry by taking a break back home. To that effect, he utters confessions such as 'I'm going back to the family / 'Cause I've had about all I can take' with a degree of welcoming and earnest compassion. One can only imagine how he would have felt – or now feels – in the age of modern technology and relentlessly voyeuristic and sensationalised journalism. Nonetheless, but it's easy to empathise with and admire Anderson's blunt daydream revelations all the same.

The rest of the troupe back him up exceptionally, with plenty of urbane changes throughout. Bunker, Cornick, and Barre start out with simple cymbal taps and patterns, respectively, before the chorus ignites a livelier deviation of flute and drumming freak-outs. This duality guides the track, of course, with that initial motif acting as a reassuring sense of familiarity henceforth. Naturally, Barre steals the spotlight near the end with a scorching solo, finishing off the band's most multi-layered and ambitious arrangement to date.

'Look into the Sun' (Anderson)

In plain contrast to its predecessor, this is a splendidly pastoral and poetic acoustic ballad that, perhaps more than any other inclusion on Stand Up, points towards the poignant sentiments of 1970's Benefit. Its music is appropriately dignified and sombre – rather than notably ornate – with only soft guitar and piano chords and leads comforting Anderson's gloomy thoughts ('So when you look into the sun / And see the things we haven't done / Oh was it better then to run / Than to spend the summer crying?'). It's a wonderful example of his prowess as a singer and lyricist. Beyond that, and as any fan of forlorn tunes knows, it's the lingering sparseness of the instrumentation that makes it so effective; thus, it's a testament to their collective wisdom that they learned that lesson so early on.

'Nothing is Easy' (Anderson)

From the get-go, this one is conquered by Anderson's punchy woodwind theatrics, and it's all the better for it. While still channelling a tad of their former blues DNA and simple rhyming schemes, there's no denying the heightened techniques on display here, with a sustained intensity and haste being fulfilled by irregular rhythmic shifts (especially regarding the start-and-stop tendencies Bunker and Cornick proffer throughout it). The first half is striking enough with its impassioned verses, panicked percussion, and fiery six-string fills, but it's during the latter portion that the quartet's increased dynamics and intricacy ultimately shine. Everyone gets a chance to pull out all the stops, as both Barre and Anderson let loose in-between some truly dizzying drum feats and humbly suitable bass counterpoints. It's an exquisite example of how well they reinforced and motivated each other as a unit, as well as the almost irrefutable start of Jethro Tull as a progressive rock ensemble.

'Fat Man' (Anderson)

Centring even more on Eastern influences than 'Jeffrey Goes to Leicester Square', 'Fat Man' immediately divulges Anderson's desire to expand and explore the boundaries of what rock music can be. Explicitly, his use of rapid mandolin surges, coupled with Bunker's bongo and bell ingenuity, makes it a highly distinguished, fresh, and bold venture that sits comfortably alongside earlier stylistic fusions (for instance, The Beatles 'Tomorrow Never Knows', The Byrds' 'Eight Miles High', and The Rolling Stones' 'Paint It Black'). One final thing: contrary to popular belief, the song isn't meant as a jab against Mick Abrahams. In a chat with *Music Aficionado*, Anderson clarifies as much while conceding that Abrahams was 'chubby' and that the misunderstanding 'just added another nail in the coffin of [their] relationship'.

'We Used to Know' (Anderson)

Colder and fuller than 'Look into the Sun', it's a gorgeously wistful ode about times gone by (as Cornick conveyed to It's Psychedelic Baby! Magazine, it deals with the difficult life he and Anderson had before the group. At that point they 'lived in Luton in the worst little apartments you ever saw and ... were so poor that [they] would share one can of stew or soup ... each evening'). Rarely, if ever, had Anderson captured longing heartache better in his singing and lyricism, with several stanzas – 'Could be soon we'll cease to sound / Slowly upstairs, faster down / Then to revisit stony grounds / We used to know' – also showcasing more sophisticated wordplay (namely, alliteration).

Luckily, the music does the songwriting justice. Beginning with just some acoustic guitar strums and dim electric guitar complements, Bunker and Cornick soon imbue more oomph with their waltz pace, leading to a charismatic flute solo – and multiple wah-wah guitar eruptions – cementing the emotional weight of the work. It's handsomely devastating on all accounts.

'Reasons for Waiting' (Anderson)
The whimsical mixture of acoustic guitar, dual woodwinds, and organ makes it a charmingly pacifying addition that evokes similar passages from Led Zeppelin (no doubt because both were enthused by English folk singer/ songwriter Roy Harper). There's a timeless and universal quality to its spirit that makes it instantly enticing, and the subsequent orchestral treatment – as well as the sporadic bursts of drama – make it one of the strongest moments on Stand Up, no question.

'For a Thousand Mothers' (Anderson) Whereas 'Round' ended This
Was on a short and placid note, 'For a Thousand Mothers' is a bombastic finale that once again centres on Anderson's autobiographical ponderings. As opposed to the friendliness of 'Back to the Family', however, it's quite antagonistic ('Did you hear father? / Calling my name into the night / Saying I'll never be what I am now / Telling me I'll never find what I've already found / It was they who were wrong'). Visibly, he was using his songwriting as a means of exorcising his internal conflicts.

Musically, it's extraordinarily advanced from the start, with an odd time signature steering a cacophony of hurried overlapping timbres. Obviously, Bunker and Cornick dominate as a coordinated duo bent on supplying fascinating tension; elsewhere, Anderson proves relentless in his flute flourishes, and while Barre by and large plays it straight, his infrequent attacks have great bearing nonetheless. Overall, it's a masterfully hypnotic and ruthless gem that leaves you yearning and prepared for the benefits to come.

Bonuses
'Living in the Past' (Anderson)
'Living in the Past' – which would become Jethro Tull's first Top 40 hit in the US in 1972 – was recorded before Stand Up and logically remains one of their most beloved early offerings. It's incredibly catchy, jovial, and fluid both vocally and musically, with the band's leisurely folk/jazz backbone (including odd time signatures) enticing you beneath Anderson's tunefully friendly narration. Decades later, it's as absorbing as ever.

In addition to a stereo version of *Stand Up*, the 2016 'Elevated Edition' includes stereo and 5.1 surround mixes, plus some BBC session tracks and clips from Jethro Tull's January 9th, 1969 concert at the Stockholm

Konserthuset. There are also a couple of amusing radio spots and four non-album cuts. These include: 'Martin's Tune' (a lengthy instrumental collage), 'To Be Sad is a Mad Way to Be' (a fast and bluesy rocker), 'Driving Song' (another fast and bluesy rocker), and most famously, 'Living in the Past'. Cumulatively, the 'Elevated Edition' is a robust must-own set for any devotee.

Benefit (1970)

Personnel:
Ian Anderson: vocals, acoustic guitar, electric guitar (6), flute, keyboards, balalaika
Martin Barre: electric guitar,
Clive Bunker: drums, percussion
Glenn Cornick: bass guitar, Hammond organ
Dee Palmer: orchestral arrangements
John Evan: piano and organ
Robin Black: engineer
Ruan O'Lochlainn: cover design, photography
Produced at Morgan Studios, London, September 1969 – February 1970 by Ian Anderson and Terry Ellis
UK release date: April 1970. US release date: May 1970.
Highest chart places: UK: 3, USA: 11
Running time: 42:49
Current edition: Rhino 2013 two-CD/one DVD 'Collector's Edition' (Steven Wilson Remixed)

After the rich creative and commercial successes of Stand Up, it's fair to say that that expectations were upstretched for their 1970 follow-up. As Barre remembered in a conversation with Classic Rock Revisited, though, they were more than up for the task; in fact, while he was 'terrified' being the newcomer on Stand Up, he and the rest of the gang felt 'confident' and 'at ease' making Benefit because of how accomplished and well received that second sequence was. Predictably, that self-assurance and maturity bleed into every part of Benefit's outstanding power and unity, making it a deeply private, beguiling, and cohesive declaration that demonstrably solidified their transition from blues-rock darlings to hard/folk rock emissaries.

On the surface, it follows the emphasis on heavy guitar riffs perpetuated by peers like Cream, Led Zeppelin, Black Sabbath, Deep Purple, Jimi Hendrix, Blue Oyster Cult, Traffic, etc. As a consequence, Barre stands out more by filling the tracks with technical grandeur and malevolent subtext. The remaining trio up their game, too, to make it a significantly hostile creation whose softer moments are then made even more tempting precisely because of how majestically they balance that aggression. It's an impeccable end result.

Benefit also marks the final appearance of Cornick and the first of pianist – and Anderson's pre-Jethro Tull bandmate – John Evan (although he wasn't an official member yet). Of the former circumstance, it's pretty simple: Cornick's 'party animal' persona put him at odds with the 'reclusive and insular nature of the other guys' rather private and atypical lifestyles'. Such disparity, coupled with his disagreements with Anderson over the direction of Benefit, led producer Terry Ellis to 'invite' Cornick to leave the group and start his own band (which would become Wild Turkey). As for Evan's involvement, he heard 'Living in the Past' on the radio while in college and was intrigued because of its 'unusual time signature for a pop song'. Since he and Anderson were neighbours at the time, Anderson invited him to do some sessions with them – and eventually forgo his studies entirely to become a full member – leading to a whole new level of possibilities.

Going back to the essence of the record, it's widely regarded as a darker turn for them thematically as well. At the time, Anderson felt irritated by the music business and extensive touring in the US, sparking an innately jaded and disconcerted disposition (that would be even more pronounced on 1971's landmark Aqualung). According to Cornick, Benefit deals primarily with Anderson's affections for his first wife, Jennie Franks (which Anderson later denied), and the common subject of his complicated rapport with his parents. While its inspirations and content are still debated, there's certainly something there that makes Anderson react comparatively coldly toward it, concluding that he doesn't 'identify' or feel happy with much of the material anymore.

Although its mastermind now somewhat dismisses Benefit, Barre has reverence for it and Cornick deems it his favourite of the whole bunch. Despite doing nearly as well in the UK and better in the US chart-wise, it received lacklustre feedback when it came out (primarily for not representing as great a leap from its predecessor as Stand Up did from This Was, which is contentious, to say the least). Ironically, it's commonly viewed today as the best of the Cornick era and a crucial link to their landmark fourth studio statement.

'With You There to Help Me' (Anderson)
Supposedly written about Jennie Franks and Anderson's desire to have some relief from life on the road, 'With You There to Help Me' sets the stage with (and then maintains) an ethereal sonic whirlwind of flutes, piano notes, and moans (accomplished via reverse recording, demonstrating how *Benefit* also pushed Jethro Tull production-wise). From there, acoustic guitar chords and controlled rhythms present a morose yet relaxing choral chant before his multitracked vocals ensnare with embittered soliloquies. Already, the album's darker tone – musically and narratively – is arrestingly apparent; similarly, Barre's periodic flareups display pre-eminent panache, as if he's staking his claim as a guitar legend right then and there. Truthfully, these first two minutes alone expose how much tighter, bolder, and more experimental *Benefit* is – and we haven't even gotten to its extra shift into a somewhat brighter chorus and arrangement. It's an ingeniously tumultuous way to kick off a record and declare newfound stylistic supremacy.

'Nothing to Say' (Anderson)
The central guitar refrains – mirrored perfectly by Cornick – and subjugated verses make this a quintessential Jethro Tull ballad. In particular, the sympathetic heft of Anderson's immensely eloquent and touching words ('Every morning pressure forming all around my eyes / Ceilings crash, the walls collapse, broken by the lies / That your misfortune brought upon us

and I won't disguise them') are made even more sublimely distressing and enterprising by acoustic arpeggios, Evan's accompaniments, and Anderson's closing chants. In terms of sheer unbridled emotion and sincerity, its dystopic existentialism –or is it about unresolved romance? – yields his best performance thus far while synchronously hinting at the social commentaries he'd latter investigate. (Interestingly, Barre recalls that 'Nothing to Say' was the first time he and Anderson shared guitar duties: 'I played fingerstyle and Ian played plectrum').

'Alive and Well and Living In' (Anderson)
Signifying the first of several differences between the UK and US versions of Benefit, this third selection only appears on the British edition (for whatever reason, 'Inside' was moved up five spots in America to replace it). At first, Evan chimes in with an elegantly mysterious foundation on which Anderson reports his perceptions about a sovereign and overlooked woman. In-between, Bunker, Evan, and Barre interrupt with quirky breaks, setting Anderson's fervent choruses ablaze. Naturally, there's an abundance of soaring woodwinds as well, and near the end, Barre and Evan align their solos to aid the sumptuous classiness of the whole arrangement. In general, it's a superbly tasteful and go-getting composition full of attractive ideas.

'Son' (Anderson)
Continuing the familial focus Stand Up, 'Son' is a rousing tour-de-force of conflicting tones and astute conversational songwriting. Following the genial ending of 'Alive and Well and Living In', it begins explosively with Barre's imposing riff smothering you without a second to breathe. He flawlessly assists Anderson, who – as Father – sends stern echoed lectures about youthful disrespect and unappreciation, setting up a dazzlingly novel and incongruous shift to his defiant but anxious role as Son, whose almost Shakespearean coming-of-age quandaries perfectly capture the disenfranchised duty of adolescence. Complementarily, Barre's plucked intervals emulate Anderson's melody with stark care, joining Evan's chords for a stunning philosophical aside before the piece returns home with awesome instrumental vigour and sobering banter. Undoubtedly, the superlative lyric of them all is 'You've only turned thirty / so son, you'd better apologise / And when you grow up / If you're good, we will buy you a bike' because it single-handedly dismisses their power struggle by implying that no matter how much of an adult the boy becomes, he will always be a child to his parents. Thus, Anderson speaks volumes about a generation gap in a single verse. That he was merely twenty-two when Jethro Tull completed the track makes its concise wisdom even more clever. Likewise, its recursive heavy-light-heavy route was a divergent touchstone that overtly led to successive staples throughout the decade (such as 'Aqualung', 'Thick as a Brick', and 'Baker Street Muse').

'For Michael Collins, Jeffrey and Me' (Anderson)

The concluding chapter of the Jeffrey Hammond trilogy, it's also dedicated to astronaut Michael Collins (who piloted the Command Module Columbia while Neil Armstrong and Buzz Aldrin walked on the moon). Specifically, it's Anderson's way of paying tribute to Collins as a relatively unsung part of the troupe. He describes what Collins may have seen and felt vividly and tenderly, contrasting defeated singing and abstract imagery – abetted by sorrowful arpeggios and scant percussion – in the verses with inspired inferences and palpable comradery – abetted by a full-bodied arrangement – in the choruses. As such, both the music and vocals expertly convey polarised outlooks (as if to convey Collins' cognitive dissonance between abandonment and persistence). Taking into account that Evan and Anderson were now playing together again, it's easy to see the parallel amid Collins and Hammond as the odd men out of their formative trio.

'To Cry You a Song' (Anderson)

Another raucous rocker, 'To Cry You a Song' is arguably the most immediately fetching part of Benefit due to Barre's skulking bite (which he admits was partially a nod to Blind Faith's 'Had to Cry Today') and Anderson's deliciously snarky singing. It's said to be about Anderson's agitation at going through airport customs and flying home ('Search in my case / Can't find what they're looking for'), only to have that restlessness assuaged once he returns from 'driving through London town' and sees Jennie Franks 'peeping through curtains drawn' and watching him arrive home with a 'smile in [her] eyes [that] was never so sweet before'. While they've always made a very fitting pair, the ways in which Barre's licks support Anderson's lashings is chiefly impactful here. Once again, Bunker and Cornick match them with a start-and-stop pattern (alongside Barre) that makes it even more mesmeric.

'A Time for Everything?' (Anderson)

Moving away from the angry vibe of the prior number, 'A Time for Everything?' is prettily folky and nostalgic. It's as if Anderson imagines himself at middle-age, contemplating where his life went. Sure, it's transparently pensive – with a slight air of regret in his character – but it's surprisingly buoyant and welcoming at the same time, allowing his flute to dance around the elastic drums, reverberated guitar (that switches between copying Anderson's motifs and doing its own thing), and jubilant piano. Paradoxically, its weathered storytelling is disputed by its exuberant and moderately freeform (at least near the end) instrumentation, causing an interesting survey of opposites.

'Inside/Teacher' (Anderson)

Like the third slot in the sequence, this eighth one was different in the UK (where 'Inside' sat) and in the US (where 'Teacher' presided). Tackling the former first, it's positively surreal and carnivalistic in its maiden measures, where the eccentric array of celebratory woodwinds, playful six-string slides, twirling bass cycles, and backward beats unite in peculiar counterpoints. Anderson carries that sunny outlook verbally, too, by relishing in the basic pleasures of life (such as cups of coffee, walking, companionship, etc.) with a tone of contentment and catharsis. It makes sense, then, that a wealth of aficionados see 'Inside' as the calm after the storm (or darkness) that saturated much of what preceded it. After all, there have been a lot of tears shed thus far, so it's nice to finally discover Anderson feeling 'glad' to 'enjoy life again'.

'Teacher' also presents an upbeat attitude to battle Benefit's earlier grievances. For example, the chorus is warm and fun-loving ('Jump up, look around / Find yourself some fun / No sense in sitting there hating everyone'), and the fusion of cheery bass rotations, vibrant keyboard chirps, energised syncopation, thrilled flute floods, and tranquil guitar noodling boosts the magnetism. As Anderson revealed to Songfacts, he wrote it that way to 'get [them] some radio play or be in the singles charts' (which it was, placing at #4 with its A-side, 'Witch's Promise'). Its subject matter, on the other hand, has a more profound meaning than many listeners may think. The song seems on the surface to be inspired by Evan's parents (his mother taught piano and his father was a retired school instructor), yet in chatting with UnmaskUs, Anderson illuminates that it's actually an indictment of 'those creepy guru figures that would mislead innocent young minds' in order to amass money and control. Like 'A Time for Everything?', its explicit happiness is a stark juxtaposition to its shadier stimulus.

'Play in Time' (Anderson)
Frankly, the simplistic direction of 'Play in Time', although quite good, would make it feel like a step back if not for the nightmarishly psychedelic effects of its sped-up guitarwork and tape manipulation. In fact, Anderson seems to acknowledge this when he belts out, 'Blues were my favourite colour / 'Til I looked around and found another song / That I felt like singing'. It basically boils down to a candid – though rhythmically demanding – beast whose militaristic brashness is intercepted by those avant-garde properties. Despite being the least essential portion of *Benefit,* its concoctions make it quite worthwhile nevertheless.

'Sossity; You're a Woman' (Anderson)
Right away, this closer establishes a sullen tenor with its combination of funereal organ notes and layered acoustic guitar constructions (that skilfully move around Anderson's dirges about the 'disdain ... [he] might have felt for people who would display wealth and authority without having earned it'). Halfway through, his words are abruptly and harrowingly stifled by tambourines, flutes, and more organ; this dichotomy repeats again before Barre's finishes with an emotive chromatic ascension. As with erstwhile odes, it's the bareness and conviction that ultimately makes it so effective. Beyond

itself, 'Sossity; You're a Woman', with its allegorical pun of turning 'society' into 'a rather prissy girls' name', returns Benefit to its darker spirit after the former pieces acted like metaphorical lights at the end of the tunnel. In that way, it cements Benefit as their most resolute, evocative, and mature LP of the Cornick period.

Bonuses
'Sweet Dream'(Anderson)
A threatening and seductive leftover from the *Stand Up* sessions (that peaked at #7 in the UK charts), 'Sweet Dream' is ceaselessly captivating (especially with its boisterous strings and horns). Barre's iconic riff alone makes it a classic – as does Anderson's robust singing – and the fusion of electric, acoustic, and classical touches is apropos yet ambitious and prophetic. Thus, it worked for the time while also demonstrating how much Jethro Tull – like most popular contemporaries – were always thinking about the next evolution.

'The Witches Promise' (Anderson)
'The Witch's Promise' is an orchestrated slice of rustic opulence that signalled the direction of *Songs from the Wood* a few years later. It gained momentum after being featured on Top of the Pops and still sounds ahead of its time (due in part to Evan's distinctive debut contributions). As usual, its acoustic arpeggios and woodwind movements are obvious treats, and Bunker's reserved precision is a crucial aspect, too. It's tracks like this that show what makes early Jethro Tull so singular.

Steven Wilson's 2013 'Collector's Edition' is analogous to his 2016 submission for *Stand Up*. For the most part, it consists of stereo and 5.1 surround mixes of the album, as well as a couple more radio spots, mono versions of selected songs, and even the UK and US versions of 'Teacher'. As usual, it's the bonus tracks that truly excite. These included are the European single of 'Sweet Dream'/'17'. Also included is 'Witch's Promise'. As you'd expect, it's the complete treatment *Benefit* deserves.

Aqualung (1971)

Personnel:
Ian Anderson: vocals, acoustic guitar, flute
Martin Barre: electric guitar, descant recorder
Clive Bunker: drums, percussion
Jeffrey Hammond-Hammond: bass guitar, alto recorder, backing vocals (4)
John Evan: piano, organ, mellotron
Dee Palmer: orchestral arrangements and conducting
John Burns: engineer
Burton Silverman: album artwork
Produced at Island Studios, London, December 1970 – February 1971 by Ian
Anderson and Terry Ellis
UK and US release date: March 1971.
Highest chart places: UK: 4, USA: 7
Running time: 42:55
Current edition: Rhino 2016 two-CD/two DVD 'Anniversary Adapted Edition'
(Steven Wilson Remixed)

As we've examined, Jethro Tull's first three assemblages were invaluable in
helping the group reach a nearly unparalleled blend of extensive artistic
growth, critical praise, and public favour. That said, they're also somewhat
assessed in retrospect as stepping stones towards what would become the
band's most illustrative – and biggest-selling – effort ever: 1971's *Aqualung*.
A reasonable yet vast progression (pun intended) from *Benefit* all-around,
it pressed the quintets musicianship into even more miscellaneous and
technical territories in the midst of introducing a new plateau of contentious
intellectualism to Anderson's personal and ardent observations. Nearly fifty
years later, *Aqualung* denotes the formal realisation of Jethro Tull into both a
progressive folk band and, with its remarkably recognisable names (especially
'Aqualung' and 'Locomotive Breath'), a classic/stadium rock standard.

Internally and externally, *Aqualung* is daring and divisive in terms of what
larger messages, if any, it bears. Outside of the shady dealings discussed in
the opening duo, the emphasis on theology during the last five entries has
led numerous connoisseurs to deem it an intentional – and accordingly,
pioneering –concept album. However, Anderson has always vehemently
rejected that interpretation, calling it 'just a bunch of songs' that 'have some
sympathy for each other'. The official website adds further elucidation by
estimating that it's 'arguably [their] most misunderstood album' with 'a
dominant theme but [it] is certainly ... much more than a concept album
hinging on a solitary subject'. This confusion, among other things, geared
Anderson to satirise concept albums as a form with 1972's *Thick as a
Brick* (and, ironically enough, create one of the greatest of all time, but
we'll get to that). Regardless of which stance you side with, *Aqualung*'s
fearless and academic dig into such cogitations was relatively, if not wholly,

unprecedented at the time, so it was ground-breaking either way.

Equally trailblazing were the album's elaborate and sundry scores. Yes, Jethro Tull tipped their feet into the progressive rock pool before (including multipart structures), but this is conclusively where they took the complete dive. No doubt, the official addition of Evan was a major component, as was the replacement of Cornick with Hammond (so, pleasantly, the schoolyard trio was now totally reunited, with Hammond doubling his surname for creative/professional purposes). With a fuller line-up, everyone felt compelled and safe to aim farther toward genre-defying intricacy and a chameleonic palate.

Aqualung also has one of the most famed covers of the decade. As Anderson tells it, Silverman's watercolour portrait was based on a photograph that Jennie Franks – now Jennie Anderson – had taken during college, when she was 'very much into tramps, very much into dirty old men'. She snapped a handful of pictures on the Thames Embankment of 'this particular guy, who was a very striking figure' with 'defiance' and 'a nobility about him'. Over the decades, Anderson has come to dislike the final image, perceiving the painting as unattractive and shoddy – as well as looking too much like him back then – and wishing that they'd used Jennie's actual photo instead.

It's true that *Aqualung* lacks a bit of the focus and charm of *Benefit* (and, to an extent, *Stand Up*), yet that's exactly why it's such an evolution. Far deeper and more ambitious musically, it instantaneously tested their fanbase, increased their draw, and broke new ground for what a rock band could do and say. In other words, the troupe's previous catalogue set the stage for this fourth outing; *Aqualung* set the stage not only for every Jethro Tull album to follow but also for the legion of progressive folk proteges to arise in its aftermath. It's almost unanimously considered their crowning work (it's their top assortment of tracks, at least), and even if devotees prefer another option, it's practically guaranteed that when casual/mainstream audiences think of Jethro Tull, they think of *Aqualung*.

'Aqualung' (Anderson, Jennie Anderson)

Arguably Jethro Tull's most characteristic and revered composition, there's little new to say about this gem (but let's try anyway). The track is an overtly socially conscious ode about the plight of the homeless, including society's disgraceful response to them. The song's lyrics were co-written by Jennie Anderson and they do an excellent job of portraying its namesake as both sleazy ('Sitting on a park bench / Eying little girls with bad intent / Snot's running down his nose / Greasy fingers smearing shabby clothes') and sympathetic ('Sun streaking cold / An old man wandering lonely / Taking time, the only way he knows'). It's a level of vivid imagery unlike what they'd done before, and the ways in which Anderson delivers these lines is similarly weighty, oscillating between raspy schadenfreude (with a cackle or two) and pitied distance like a masterful storyteller. He's always been an excellent singer, but this is the first time he became a thespian as well (which correlates to his onstage get-ups and antics around this time, too).

Of course, few guitar riffs in the genre are as justly iconic as Barre's recurrent outbreak, nor are there many solos that could rival his meticulously organised opus (recorded as Jimmy Page stood in the control room, waving and inciting him to give it his all). Around him, Evan, Hammond-Hammond, and Bunker keep it forthright (albeit with lovely ascending piano chords) until Anderson's hectic, yet mournful capo'd acoustic guitar (itself a trademark) leads to a reprise of the opening that allows for some very tricky syncopation. Despite each segment being strong enough to stand on its own, it's the seamlessness with which they're tied as a three-part structure (that comes full circle upon completion) that makes 'Aqualung' so thrilling, touching, and innovative. Although it was never released as a single because it was 'too long' and 'episodic', it remains one of the most enduring rock songs of the 1970s and has even been used as an official pseudonym by English singer/songwriter Matthew Hales).

'Cross-Eyed Mary' (Anderson)
Considering its direct connection to the previous tune, it's no wonder that people think this is a concept album. To be sure, this second selection once again revolves around a dissolute person (in this case, a schoolgirl prostitute) who's meant to embody how all of 'God's creations' possess 'essential humanity ... [and] goodness'. In fact, Anderson compares her altruism – she'll provide her services to clients who can't afford them – to that of Robin Hood. Even so, there's a disturbing ugliness to the world around her (such as the 'jack-knife barber', or abortionist, 'who 'drops her off at school') that additionally demonstrates the richer and more invasive moral dilemmas scattered throughout *Aqualung*. Aptly, if also shockingly, Anderson has never seemed so destructive; his resonance is downright razor sharp as he barks his sordid anecdotes, and he builds up to it with a haunting flute introduction (assisted by tiptoeing rhythms and a suspenseful synth atmosphere). Barre evokes a melodic chainsaw the whole time as well, lending even more wicked appeal to an otherwise straightforward turn.

'Cheap Day Return' (Anderson)
In contrast to the acrimonious qualities of the starting twosome, 'Cheap Day Return' is a brief acoustic elegy Anderson wrote about taking a trip to see his ill father, as is the similar closing of the *Life is a Long Song* EP, 'Nursie', which was released near the end of 1971. As he puts it, they'd just started mending their relationship and, because he was quite far away, he was eager to see his father and avoid feeling 'very much cut up at being denied the opportunity to make [his] final farewell'. Despite its dim, bittersweet dignity (brought forth by delicate arpeggios and strings), it's not a morbid piece; rather, its slice-of-life bemusement at a hospitable nurse who asked for Anderson's autograph is sweetly telling of how we cherish the flukes of life that rest on top of the burdens.

'Mother Goose' (Anderson)

Distancing himself further from the heavy sounds and subjects that began *Aqualung*, Anderson jumps fully into the festive and fanciful with this fetching number. He sings merrily about 'walk[ing] by Hampstead Fair' and encountering figures like Long-John Silver, the bearded lady, Johnny Scarecrow, and more while also alluding to the 'Sing a Song of Sixpence' nursery rhyme; in doing so, he creates his own highly detailed and entrancing fairy-tale out of the others. (There's also the reference to 'at least a hundred schoolgirls sobbing into handkerchiefs' that subtly links the track to 'Cross-Eyed Mary'). As the middle portion of Aqualung's sequential acoustic trilogy (with some electric guitar as well), 'Mother Goose' lovingly counterparts his verses with victorious flutes, forceful chords, intricate plucking, organic percussion, and even some fresh backing vocals from Hammond-Hammond. Overall, it's a very cordial entry that helps offset the surrounding chaos and, in effect, represents how Jethro Tull were forging new ground with the record as a whole.

'Wond'ring Aloud' (Anderson)

Borne from the ashes of 'Wond'ring Again' (which was recorded during the Benefit tour in July 1970), it fits in nicely with Anderson's other beautiful and commanding ballads. It's likely his most heart-warming yet, too, as its gentle nature lends itself perfectly to tender accounts of domesticated romance ('She floats in the kitchen / I'm tasting the smell / Of toast as the butter runs / Then she comes, spilling crumbs on the bed'). Evan's piano frolics and Palmer's symphonic retorts inherently add even more summery splendour, and beyond its 'personal nonsense' (as he described to *Disc and Music Echo* in 1971), it's another hopeful break from the nastiness sightseen elsewhere on the album. In the same interview, Anderson called 'Wond'ring Aloud' 'the most satisfying thing I've made a record of', and all these years later, it remains one of his most life-affirming and regal gifts.

'Up to Me' (Anderson)

'Up to Me' finishes off the first side of *Aqualung* by returning to the compelling antipathy of *Benefit* (with a more multifarious arrangement). In particular, the speaker (another miscreant) boasts about his egocentrism with every stanza, spouting out first-person instructions about a date, a bar fight, affluence, and more. He seems desperate to have someone else indulge in his memories and threats, and since he's 'a common working man with half a bitter, bread, and jam', it's unclear how much he's embellishing his chronicle. Regardless, there's a definite liberty to his life; unshackled by the constraints of civilised culture, he's permitted to do as he places, embodying the notion that 'It's only after you've lost everything that you're free to do anything' (as Chuck Palahniuk writes in *Fight Club*).

From start to finish, the scoundrel's gloats are fenced by resentful riffs, flutes, and drums that periodically give way to peaceful respites (decorated by

Bunker's inventive drumming). Hence, the development of the timbres is as engaging as the development of the narration, reinforcing how Jethro Tull were testing new waters within a formation that could've belonged to the preceding album. What's also interesting is the reference to 'a Wimpy Bar', as the restaurant is also mentioned in Genesis' 'Dancing with the Moonlight Knight' two years later. Ubiquitous in the UK, Wimpy bars were hamburger restaurants in the American style well before Burger King or McDonalds found their way out of the USA. They had a sort of down at heel notoriety at the time.

'My God' (Anderson)
Just as the title track kindled its titular side in volatile fashion, so too does 'My God' with its concluding suite. Beginning with tense acoustic fingerpicking, it soon melds into the central melody (with added piano) as Anderson ruefully asks, 'People, what have you done? / Locked Him in His golden cage / Golden cage / Made Him bend to your religion'. Right away, the song captures an appropriately accusatory and solemn tenor that contrasts well its livelier – though still critical – answer: 'He is the God of nothing / If that's all that you can see'. It's not long before Barre's electric part explodes on top (as do the rest of the band), igniting awesome dynamics around Anderson's crotchety denouncements. His midway solo is among his most memorable, too, especially in how the rest of the score fades beneath it to highlight his exasperated urgency prior to a dramatic multi-layered duel between spiritual chants and woodwind flights of fancy (that, looking back, point to the ingenious bizarreness of *A Passion Play*). As on other sections of *Aqualung*, this deviation eventually resolves home to end the journey, leaving listeners winded, meditative, and thoroughly captivated.

Contrary to surface level interpretations, 'My God' isn't an all-encompassing anti-theology rant. Instead, it's a scathing indictment of the hypocrisy, conformity, and abuse of power behind universal worship (including 'the bloody Church of England'). Anderson clarifies, 'It's very dissatisfying to me that children are brought up to follow the same God as their parents', adding that God is merely 'the abstract idea Man chooses to worship' and that traditional faith 'makes a dividing line between human beings' that prevents people from having their own interpretations and conclusions without fear of judgement. Whether you agree or disagree with those views, you have to commend his gallantry in boundlessly confronting such a controversial topic; similarly, the whole ensemble warrants praise for crafting such a complex and transformative aural experience.

'Hymn 43' (Anderson)
Bursting with almost light-hearted rambunctiousness via hoarse singing, combustible riffs, scuffling syncopation, and springy piano chords, this descendant takes a more fun and slightly tongue-in-cheek approach to

criticising organised doctrine. Its catchy chorus – 'If Jesus saves, well He'd better save Himself / From the gory glory seekers who use His name in death' – blatantly admonishes opportunists, deceivers, and like-minded folk who cite Christianity as a means to profit or excuse wrongdoing. It's interesting, then, to consider how Anderson may be intentionally and ironically playing one of the self-righteous leaders he's chastising as he presents his proclamations. Musically, it feels a bit like a pastiche of 1950s American rock and roll, and its argument (about sinister misrepresentations of Christ) paved the way for countless thematic siblings in its wake (namely, Ben Folds' 'Jesusland' and XTC's 'Dear God').

'Slipstream' (Anderson)

The third acoustic interlude of the set, 'Slipstream' is quite similar to 'Wond'ring Aloud' (maybe to a fault), but its sparser persona and hopeful nature – about finding peace in the afterlife and abandoning material things – makes it a valuable inclusion nonetheless. The peculiar orchestral swirl at the end is an interesting touch as well, and the whole idea of looking back on your life once you've passed away is a definite previewing of the drama within A Passion Play.

'Locomotive Breath' (Anderson)

The other huge hit from Aqualung, it takes a more carefree tactic to explore death after 'the unending train journey of life'. Evan's classical-to-blues piano opening is instantly seizing – as are Barre's cool licks, which fade into his main pattern and muted strikes (representing the trudge of a monorail) adeptly. Behind him, Bunker provides many nifty fills as Hammond-Hammond sustains an essential groove. Upfront, Anderson sings with hostile glee, using the title and lyrics as metaphors for the 'claustrophobic feel of a lot of people in a limited space ... [and] the unstoppable population expansion on planet Earth'. For example, 'Old Charlie stole the handle' refers to God being unable (or unwilling) to stop what Man has done, choosing instead just to watch it all unfold (which sort of relates to Deism). Suitably, he unleashes one of his most topsy-turvy flute solos to date during the commotion.

It was recorded atypically by overdubbing various parts together (like Anderson's hi-hat and bass drum contributions) because he couldn't get a proper recreation of his vision in a joint recording session. Distributed as a single in the US and Europe (but not the UK), it has become one of Jethro Tull's most frequently played songs on FM radio. It's also among their most covered tunes, with reimagined takes from Rabbitt (on 1975's *Boys Will Be Boys*), W.A.S.P. (as a bonus on the reissue of 1989's *The Headless Children*), Styx (on 2005's Big Bang Theory), and Helloween (on 1999's *Metal Jukebox*), among others. It was even used as the name of a Swedish rock band formed by guitarist Janne Stark. Clearly, the train still hasn't slowed down.

'Wind-Up' (Anderson)

In a 1990 American interview ('In the Studio – *Aqualung*'), Anderson explains how the title of this last one refers to three things simultaneously. Firstly it refers to the finishing off of the LP. Secondly, it refers to the connected belief that one shouldn't trick God by going to church only on Sundays. Finally, he cites the difficulty of ignoring him the rest of the week or the need to invoke him once a week to ensure his constant presence. It's the latter two messages that make 'Wind Up' both poignant and cumulatively resounding as the final thoughts on *Aqualung's* most prevalent theme. It specifically harkens back to 'My God' in its depiction of a child being indoctrinated into religion by his elders and then attempting to get the truth behind the Almighty. Its most significant lines – 'I don't believe you / You had the whole damn thing all wrong / He's not the kind you have to wind up on Sundays' – do an excellent job of portraying that thesis (as well as implying that even the most smugly assured are misguided because no one can *really* know the truth).

Smartly, both the vocals and instrumentation, well, 'wind-up' efficiently from defeated orthodoxy to dominant rule. At first, Anderson bemoans his upbringing alongside faint piano and acoustic guitar chords; however, the chorus brings about a renovation into rebellious empowerment that's instigated by the addition of electric six-string and steadfast percussion. Next, a double-tracked guitar bridges the way to Anderson's embraced sovereignty ('How do you dare tell me / That I'm my father's son / When that was just an accident of birth') before he repeats the first verse with newfound conviction. After riotous cheers give way to Barre letting loose against himself, 'Wind-Up' winds down to its sombre origin as if Anderson is imploring his audience to consider his lesson and follow his lead. It's yet another reason for why Aqualung was so significant at the time and remains an exemplar for the entire genre.

Bonuses

A remaster of his 2011 release (because he rebuked Peter Mew's attempt), Steven Wilson's 2016 'Anniversary Adapted Edition' offers plenty of worthy goodies. It comes with the prerequisite stereo, 5.1 surround, and quadrophonic mixes of *Aqualung*, plus 'associated recordings' from '70 and '71 like 'Lick Your Fingers Clean' (an in-your-face bit of hard rock edge), 'Just Trying to Be' (a short acoustic rhyme with pretty ornaments), and 'Wond'ring Aloud, Again' (a breathtaking merger of the two songs). Also involved is the entire *Life is a Long Song* EP, which, with its sublime title track and the funky 'For Later', is worth the price of admission alone.

Thick as a Brick (1972)

Personnel:
Ian Anderson: vocals, acoustic guitar, flute, violin, trumpet, saxophone
Martin Barre: electric guitar, lute
Barriemore Barlow: drums, percussion, timpani
Jeffrey Hammond-Hammond: bass guitar, spoken words
John Evan: piano, organ, harpsichord
Dee Palmer: orchestral arrangements
Robin Black: engineer
Roy Eldridge: album art (design; Anderson, Evan, and Hammond-Hammond
provided contents)
Produced at Morgan Studios, London, December 1971 by Ian Anderson and Terry
Ellis
UK and US release date: March 1972.
Highest chart places: UK: 5, USA: 1
Running time: 43:46
Current edition: Chrysalis 2012 CD/DVD '40th Anniversary Edition' (Steven Wilson
Remixed)

Having issued two nearly impeccable collections with *Benefit* and *Aqualung*
– each built around Anderson exorcising his personal and public concerns –
Jethro Tull decided to do something drastically different (and perhaps even
more striving and influential) with their fifth album, *Thick as a Brick*: produce
an album-long suite filled with extravagant arrangements, in-depth fictions,
and sardonic undercurrents. Demonstrating Anderson's dry and erudite sense
of humour (as well as his admiration for Monty Python), it was written as a
pointed response to both the misconception that its predecessor was a concept
album and the chief pretentiousness he saw in bands like ELP 'disappearing up
their own arses ... [with] slightly annoying spaghetti noodling and long, drawn-
out instrumental passages' (as reported by Dom Lawson in the 'Anniversary
Edition' liner notes). In other words, it found the quintet slyly shouting
to fans and critics, 'Okay, you want the Mother of all overblown prog rock
epics? We'll give it to you!' It's ironic, then, that in lampooning the template
so meticulously and imaginatively, Jethro Tull actually shaped a superlative
example of it. Without a doubt, *Thick as a Brick* took its players and its field
to new heights, resulting in another career benchmark and one of the most
multifaceted, absorbing, and prominent progressive rock tracks ever made.

Prolonged 'epic' compositions are now emblematic of the style, but at
the time, there had only been a handful of them (King Crimson's 'Lizard',
Caravan's 'Nine Feet Underground', Van der Graaf Generator's 'A Plague of
Lighthouse Keepers', and Pink Floyd's 'Echoes', for instance). Therefore, Thick
as a Brick predates – and possibly encouraged – almost every beloved staple of
its decade (including Genesis' 'Supper's Ready' and Yes' 'Close to the Edge' by
only a few months). Moreover, its place as the first 40+ minute construction in

the genre makes it a cornerstone achievement that directly drove subsequent offerings like Dream Theater's *Six Degrees of Inner Turbulence*, Fate's Warning's *A Pleasant Shade of Gray*, and Between the Buried and Me's *The Parallax II: Future Sequence*.

Of course, its duration alone would be only a nominal feat if the music within it weren't spectacularly advanced, wide-ranging, organised, and enchanting. Building upon the challenging syntheses of *Aqualung*, it concurrently expanded their formula into a new realm of virtuosic and varied magnificence – counting jazz and classical leanings – while providing 'the resonance of three-minute songs ... that you can sing along to'. Simply put, Anderson, Hammond, Evan, and Barre became even more proficient, determined, and unrestrained as musicians and collaborators, and the addition of Barriemore Barlow (who took over after Bunker got married and amicably quit) only added to their collective dexterity. Of Barlow's joining, Anderson champions how he 'really did push things on and ... raised the game for the other guys'. The band felt a purposeful camaraderie during the creation process, too, so while it was easily the toughest music they'd made so far, it was among the most enjoyable and effortless writing and recording sessions as well, featuring more input from the rest of them (especially Evan) and 'pick[ing] up its own unstoppable momentum from the start and galloped to a satisfying conclusion'.

Aside from its music, *Thick as a Brick* is quite famous for its narrative gimmick. You see, its lyrics – which, while proudly nonsensical, still draw from Anderson's insubordinate and inquisitive upbringing and relate to 'a sociological examination of a child's experience in the modern world' – were attributed as an epic poem written by a prizewinning (but then disqualified) eight-year-old prodigy named Gerald Bostock. Culturally, Anderson says that the Brits 'entered into it willingly ... because we all lived through that era of surreal British humour', whereas Americans 'found it hard to separate the fiction from reality'. Although a completely fictitious character, people still trust the hoax (which was never meant to be believed) and ask him how Bostock is doing.

To sell the Bostock ploy further, Anderson, Evan, and Hammond-Hammond – with help from Chrysalis A&R man and former local journalist, Roy Eldridge – created a comprehensive fake newspaper called The St. Cleve Chronicle & Linwall Advertiser to contain and complement the record. Apparently, it took longer to make than the music it housed, and as Anderson told Malcolm Dome in his PROG write-up 'Jethro Tull: The Story behind Thick as a Brick', they'd 'put together a lot of silly stories and also used lyrics from the album itself. [They] also got the road crew, label people and girlfriends to pose for photos.' While certain people weren't fond of such a containment (such as Terry Ellis and former Beatles John Lennon, whose similarly designed Some Time in New York City would come out a few months later and have its thunder stolen), the tactic indubitably helped get the release more attention and, in retrospect, broaden the limits of record packaging in general.

At the time, *Thick as a Brick* was met with commending, if universally mixed, reviews, yet it was also another international commercial success , earning the group their first Billboard #1 spot in the States. Today, it's widely regarded as Jethro Tull's finest hour, with artists such as Geddy Lee (Rush) and Neal Morse (of famed contemporary progressive rock bands Spock's Beard, Transatlantic) citing it as a favourite. Likewise, Anderson still has a soft spot for all it signified and accomplished (to the point that he released two solo continuations: 2012's *Thick as a Brick 2: Whatever Happened to Gerald Bostock* and 2014's *Homo Erraticus*). It's even infiltrated popular culture in recent years, including an updated appearance in a 2001 Honda commercial and a parody in an episode The Simpsons in 2006 called 'Girls Just Want to Have Sums'. For something generated as a send-up of Jethro Tull's contemporaries and critics, *Thick as a Brick* ended up as a virtually unmatched triumph in their discography and in the annals of progressive rock in total. Very few entries since have matched it – let alone surpassed it, although its heir, *A Passion Play*, is an exception – allowing it to persist as a masterpiece you definitely don't want to sit out.

'Thick as a Brick Part One' (Anderson)
The opening section was the only one written ahead of time – everything else was done during the process, with Anderson formulating new material each morning for the band to work on later that day 'like a conductor with an orchestra, trying to get the other guys to realise this masterplan'. It blends acoustic guitar arpeggios, flute, colourfully matter-of-fact rhymes, to elicit a comforting environment immediately. In contrast to the scornful ferocity found on *Aqualung*, this introductory movement harvests a welcoming dose of dynamic folk-rock.

It takes a slightly emptier and more longing turn a couple of minutes in, however, with Anderson's nostalgic request of 'Spin me back down the years and the days of my youth / Draw the lace and black curtains and shut out the whole truth'. This gives way to a showy outburst – partially in 5/4 time – of sparkling percussion, horns that emulate Anderson's prophetic melody – about imposing adult life on 'a son [who] is born' – and a fiery guitar/bass pattern that leads the whole thing. In-between, Evan and Barre exchange zany solos before theatrical spasms segue into another forlorn section (cued by marching drums, light piano, and woodwinds). Here, we're granted chilling ponderings about a poet and a painter. Just as Jethro Tull's music has already shown significant evolvement, so too have their lyrics, with lines like 'The do-er and the thinker / No allowance for the other / As the failing light illuminates the mercenary's creed' showcasing yet another step up in Anderson's knack for philosophical articulation.

After that section has been fully developed into a mournful rocker – including an essential lick and suave deviation from Barre that's zealously adorned by everyone else. A gorgeously stately troop of flutes, bass, cymbals, horns, and organ diplomatically play off of each other as they guide us into Anderson's next irresistible melody ('What do you do when the old man's gone / Do you want to be him?') highlighted by more animated drumming - Barlow is plainly and successfully eager to prove his chops.

From there, Evan chromatically ascends into and joins Anderson in fooling around a bit with one of the central motifs of *Thick as a Brick* (which is eventually cemented with gripping anticipation before Hammond-Hammond and Anderson's counterpoints flesh it out into a fascinating ride). Despite the infectious vivacity of the arrangement, Anderson recaptures a bit of his former villainy at this point by croaking cautions like 'I'll judge you all and make damn sure that no one judges me'. He subsequently ventures off into possibly his most emotionally enriched woodwind tangent to date; it's overwhelmingly effective and spellbinding (especially near the end).

As Evan offers a last refrain, acoustic guitar strums chime in and ingeniously lull the listener into a reprisal of the opening arpeggios of the track (backed by organ predictions of the next segment: a breezy detour into angelic chants). Anderson ruminates, 'You curl your toes in fun / As you smile at everyone / You meet the stares / You're unaware that your doings aren't done' alongside bells and shuffling hi-hats. It's a coolly luscious reprieve that converts – via descending piano, acoustic stabs, and flute – into more sophisticated and stern observations about 'childhood heroes' and 'join[ing] your local government' (once again detailing aspects of adolescence and adulthood). In-between, Hammond-Hammond takes charge for a moment afterwards, leading to a detonation of percussion and swarming flutes.

A punchy bridge suddenly appears ('The other kids have all backed down and they put your first in line') and is surrounded by equally persistent yet playful instrumentation. This portion is contrasted with woodwind whirlwinds (which are weighted against an alluring tug-of-war with bass/guitar) until a concluding attack of oddly timed electric guitar, piano, and bass move around an inflamed organ solo. Once it's finished, these oscillations both echo and stretch their range of volume until the left channel is nearly silent and the right is nearly deafening. Then, creeping gusts of air provide an ominous segue –

'Thick as a Brick Part Two' (Anderson)
– into the closing half of the LP. Its mirrored build-up (amidst clashing strings) invites the reappearance of a previous theme (notwithstanding Anderson now switching the son who's 'fit to fight' for a man who's 'fit for peace'). It's a clever bit of continuity – to say the least – that stresses the main commentary of *Thick as a Brick*. Similarly, Barlow's fleeting drum solo then provides a foundation on which Barre lets loose in-between flutes and bells conjuring the 'You curl your toes in fun' melody. It's here that Jethro Tull truly goes abstract, as the percussion becomes quite irregular before the whole arrangement transforming peculiarly into an unbalanced avant-garde jazz hodgepodge. In the chaos, Hammond-Hammond recites curious nonsense ('We walked through

the maternity ward and saw 218 babies wearing nylons') that spotlights the ridiculousness beneath the intricacy.

With a final cymbal tap, Barlow signals the opening acoustic guitar arpeggio's homecoming. It's nearly identical to the first moments of the LP but with more fairy-tale harmonies and woodwinds. There's also a bit more melancholic oomph as the threatening electric guitar and bass lines interject. This part glides into a dreamier offshoot in which organ, chimes, and acoustic guitar chords blanket tenderly sung words about how 'legends (worded in the ancient tribal hymn) lie cradled in the seagull's call'. Anderson sounds honourably dejected here, making it among the most effective sections in the suite.

A new acoustic keynote sparks a bucolic trip (alongside oppressed wavering effects). It's a dauntingly grave passage that's broken up by a farsighted query – 'Do you believe in the day?' – and a piercingly poignant (and faint) motif from Evan. Without a doubt, it's among the most hypnotic ideas of them all. Just as laudable is the preparation-for-battle arousal that envelops those peaceful moments, with Anderson warning, 'The Dawn Creation of the Kings has begun / Soft Venus (lonely maiden) brings the ageless one' on top of a stiff yet tempting score. This tension reaches its climax when Evan fully develops his motif into a sharp and vibrant response, generating arguably the peak of Thick as a Brick's rapture.

The quintet experiments with dynamics once more as guitar screeches and scattered keyboard and flute dance around marching syncopation. It's awesomely intense, harrowing, and eloquent, and like much of the piece, it presents a foreshadowing of the following movement in-between the current one. When it finally kicks in, it's positively delightful in its climbing energy and colourful textures. Specifically, Evan serves up a multi-layered organ celebration while the rest of the band backs him up with elastic protection (including chainsaw counterpoints from Barre). It makes for the perfect underpinning of Anderson's omniscient orders: 'Well, let me sing of the losers who lie / In the street as the last bus goes by / the pavements are empty / The gutters run red / While the fool toasts his god in the sky'.

A gutsier bypass (featuring an exhausting woodwind and harpsichord duel that Barlow and Hammond-Hammond knowledgeably manage to keep on track) steals the show afterwards. It's momentarily interrupted by another inventively lop-sided break (that includes timpani and an alarm clock) before Anderson chimes back in with rousing a calls-to-action for young men to 'join [their] voices in a hellish chorus' and 'mark the precise nature of [their] fear'. Another blithe disruption gives way to an almost gothic snippet that precedes additional cheerful virtuosity, resulting in the most difficult and resourceful instrumentation in the piece (as well as the clearest demonstration yet of how much Jethro Tull has grown as players and writers since Aqualung). It's utterly remarkable.

Unexpectedly, a robotic swirl waves a heavier variation of the 'childhood heroes' part that's then spiced up by the third appearance of the 'See there! A son is born' rhythm. Barre aids with some dazzling riffs, too, and the sudden conversion into a classical channel within the frenzy is categorically awe-inspiring. Everything comes together in a mad dash for supremacy before a dense ascension brings us home, allowing Anderson to remind us once again that 'wise men don't know how it feels to be thick as a brick'. His final chuckle now seems double-sided, as it represents the knowledge that he's pulled off his timely satire and, in hindsight, one of the greatest progressive rock compositions of all time.

Bonuses

Considering that *Thick as a Brick* is comprised of only a single two-part work, it's not surprising that the 2012 '40th Anniversary Edition' has fewer extras than its predecessors. Actually, it comes with only several versions of the album – remixed, 5.1 DTS, surround, 96/24 PCM, and a flat transfer of the original stereo mix – and a radio ad. Still, each option offers enough characteristic nuances to make absorbing all of them advisable.

A Passion Play (1973)

Personnel:
Ian Anderson: vocals, acoustic guitar, flute, soprano and sopranino saxophones
Martin Barre: electric guitar
Barriemore Barlow: drums, glockenspiel, timpani, marimba
Jeffrey Hammond-Hammond: bass guitar, vocals
John Evan: piano, organ, synthesizer, speech
Dee Palmer: orchestral arrangements
Robin Black: engineer
Brian Ward: photography
Produced at Morgan Studios, London, March 1973 by Ian Anderson and Terry Ellis
UK and US release date: July 1973.
Highest chart places: UK: 16, USA: 1
Running time: 45:05
Current edition: Chrysalis 2014 two-CD/two-DVD 'An Extended Performance'
Edition (Steven Wilson Remixed)

As urbane, demanding, and radical as *Thick as a Brick* was, it still won over
Jethro Tull fans because of its immense accessibility. Sure, it tested its architects
and audience more than any previous record conceptually and technically, but
it nonetheless earned almost united veneration for its relentlessly audacious
yet enthralling grandeur. Ironically, the exact opposite can be said about
its stylistic successor, 1973's *A Passion Play*. Far more esoteric, scholarly,
contemplative, and flat-out bizarre than the band's first foray into 40 plus
minute statements, the LP initially left many devotees feeling detached from
and disappointed by the quintet's unflinching excursion into narrative oddities
(centring on life, death, reincarnation, and the like) and darker and stranger
instrumental leaps. Fortunately, *A Passion Play* has also grown substantial
support over the past few decades, with many listeners (myself included)
deeming it superior to its forerunner. Thus, it still ranks as their most opposing
release (Anderson sees it as the 'step too far album', Evan calls it 'a downer',
and Barre reflects that they 'should have gone in a different direction'), as well
as one of the most discordant items in the whole genre. That's not surprising,
though, given its unprecedented profile. After all, *Thick as a Brick* is a
brilliantly attractive, cohesive, and multidimensional bit of music, but *A Passion
Play* – like many of the most splitting creations across all artistic mediums – is
an absolute labour of genius.

Eerily – and despite the first-time occurrence of them maintaining an
identical line-up as the last time – the project had an ominous cloud cast over
it before it had even taken proper shape. At first, the band hoped to record a
double album at Château d'Hérouville studios in France (where several notable
artists, such as Pink Floyd, Elton John, Cat Stevens, and T. Rex, had earlier
victories, although Jethro Tull's main motivation was to escape high British
tax rates). They'd recorded enough material to fill three sides of the planned

four, yet myriad difficulties – mostly living conditions, homesickness, and recording issues – forced them to scrap almost all of it, relocate to England, and start anew on what would become *A Passion Play* proper. Thankfully, that initial attempt was not a complete wash, as some ideas remained while others were rapidly salvaged elsewhere ('Only Solitaire' and 'Skating Away on the Thin Ice of the New Day' made it to 1974's *War Child*, for example). Also, more complete compilations of those sessions would appear on various 'Chateau D'Isaster Tapes' sets over time, permitting valuable lore and context to the contentious final product.

With roughly two weeks left before the next American tour, Anderson and company proved miraculously productive and capable in writing the newer music (which was 'heavily toned with dominating minor key variations'). While quite enticing once it's all internalised, there's no question that the arrangements on *A Passion Play* are significantly more perplexing and sporadic – and less user-friendly – than those on *Thick as a Brick*. Specifically, there are some Renaissance and Baroque era associations, and Anderson's notable use of sax (inspired by his childhood spent listening to Charlie Parker and Ornette Coleman) only adds to its intrepid weirdness. Of course, these wild ventures are a big part of what makes the piece so polarising (Anderson now considers it 'over-arranged and over-produced and over-cooked'), yet as PopMatters' Sean Murphy writes in his 'Ripe with Rich Attainments' retrospective, it also 'represents much of [their] finest work ... at no point was Anderson as brazen, adventurous and near-infallible as he was during the recording of A Passion Play'. Hence, even the most avid detractors should at least applaud their gusto in delivering something so fearlessly stimulating and imaginative with such haste.

Naturally, the plot and lyrics of the LP make up the other half of its somewhat vitriolic reception (and, surprisingly enough, not because its title is an explicit reference to the Passion of Jesus Christ). Whereas *Thick as a Brick* presented serious quandaries as subtext to superficial cheekiness, *A Passion Play* is upfront about its grimly metaphysical – if still madly cryptic and whimsical – storyline. Broken into four acts, it finds Anderson returning to Christianity to personify the conflict between good and evil while confronting 'the notion that choices might still be faced in the afterlife'. His vessel for the investigation is the fictional Ronnie Pilgrim, who dies in a road accident and 'passes on into a series of ... testing [and] evaluating scenarios' not unlike purgatory. (A parallel to the synopsis of Genesis' sixth outing, *The Lamb Lies Down on Broadway*, is also worth suggesting.) Fittingly, the lyrics themselves are quite opaque and dreamlike, leaving much to be interpreted by the spectator (which, admittedly, is either fascinating or frustrating depending on your point of view).

Solidifying that theatrical device is *A Passion Play*'s gleefully outlandish and divisive intermission, 'The Story of the Hare Who Lost His Spectacles'. Like Sergei Prokofiev's 1936 landmark *Peter and the Wolf* or various Lewis

Carroll odes, the interlude is a heavily orchestrated, comedic, and spirited children's tale about a group of anthropomorphic animals who try (and fail) to help their furry friend find his missing eyeglasses. Spoken by Hammond-Hammond (with an embellished Lancashire accent) and co-written by Evan, it's a startling detour to an already offbeat performance, and Jethro Tull chose to relish its absurdity visually by playing a *Wicker Man*-esque seven-minute film adaption entitled Hare (featuring ballerina Jane Eve (formerly Colthorpe) and Hammond-Hammond as a vibrant narrator with devil horns) during live renditions. Although quite maligned at the time, countless modern admirers praise its imaginative fortitude, such as Douglass Harr, who calls it 'a small masterpiece of ... hallucinatory filmmaking that's representative of the period' in his book *Rockin' the City of Angels*.

Speaking of the cover and physical contents of *A Passion Play*, it also matched, if not topped, those of *Thick as a Brick*. Featuring a haunting shot of Eve laying lifeless and upside down on an otherwise empty stage – and in front of an empty theatre – it's easily among Jethro Tull's most recognisable bits of album art. Inside is a sumptuous playbill spoof for Rena Sanderone's 'A Passion Play' (brought to life by the Linwell Players, who were just Jethro Tull under pseudonyms and matched with humorous biographical in-jokes). There were also fake credits given to positions like stage manager, chief electrician, lighting and director – as well as a stipulation that 'patrons are requested not to smoke in the auditorium' – to give the exhibition more authenticity. Of the main image, Eve told Don Needleham in the liner notes for the 'An Extended Performance' edition: 'The theme ... was death [front picture] and rebirth [back picture]. [It] was shot at the Duke of York's Theatre in St. Martin's Lane. We tried a few dead poses and I came up with the final position'. While everyone sees the line of blood dripping from her mouth, she remarks, few people ever notice the dead leaf in her left hand. Musically and visually, then, there are always new things to discover about the sequence.

Although the record and its subsequent concerts were panned by many fans and publications like *Rolling Stone*, *Melody Maker*, *Creem*, and *New Musical Express* – to the point where Terry Ellis, in a publicity stunt, told the press that Jethro Tull would go on hiatus due to the negativity – it sold well overall (especially in America). Today, *A Passion Play* is commonly seen as a textbook example of the sort of pretentious progressive rock lunacy that Anderson half-parodied (and half-bested) with *Thick as a Brick*. Of course, that pretention is wholly earned if backed up with the mind-blowing blend of skill, vision, and nerve that *A Passion Play* exudes. Anderson may joke that 'wackos ... who say that [it] is their all-time favourite album' should be confined to a mental institution, but there's plenty of justification for such a standing. At the very least, *A Passion Play* showcases a band – and genre – at their creative and technical zeniths, and that alone (and removed from subjective critiques) warrants many lovers of this black and white work of genius.

'A Passion Play Part One' (Anderson)

Subtitled 'Ronnie Pilgrim's Funeral – A Winter's Morning in the Cemetery',
the first act's introductory 'Lifebeats' instantly unveil a lingeringly unnerving
tone. Anderson's virtually inaudible soprano sax sneaks in an allusion to
a future theme beneath climbing thumps and churning dissonance. This
bedlam evolves with more boundless urgency until swirling instrumentation
and thunderous percussion summon a quirky jam of malicious festivity.
Barre and Evan double down on melodic zig-zags as Barlow and Hammond-
Hammond add some enticing rhythms before Anderson's flute motifs abduct
your attention. The quintet barrels on with ever-changing instrumentation in
a cascade of mesmerising virtuosity, that repeatedly announces snippets of
themes to come. At only three minutes in, Jethro Tull have already crafted their
most flamboyantly challenging and captivating piece to date.

A union of whistles, acoustic guitar chords, and ominous bass notes segue
into forsaken thumps and a stark crash. Anderson is then left in an empty
space to issue his grave opening line – 'Do you still see me even here? / The
silver chord lies on the ground' – as Pilgrim reflects on his demise. Gentle
guitar strums and grand piano support his recollections around 'a rush along
the Fulham Road'. Halfway through, things liven up fleetingly before going
back to the sombre ether. A final thought from Evan and Barre is met by a
few taps before an emotional marimba/keyboard loop coats the landscape
beneath an ominous swell of drums, bass, and electric guitar. Logically, it
erupts into another commanding jazz freak-out (led by Anderson's saxophone
malevolence) before venturing back with added quietude as he sings about 'a
sweetly-scented angel' coming to 'wish [him] well'. It truly feels like the first
moments of a staged drama.

Resultingly, another histrionic but sublimely colourful instrumental passage
leads into a rustic and wistful mixture of acoustic guitar and organ. Abruptly,
a stilted team-up between Barre and Barlow signifies the start of the second
act: 'The Memory Bank – A Small but Comfortable Theatre with a Cinema-
Screen (The Next Morning)'. It's not long, however, until the rest of the band
produces more multi-layered magnetism as Anderson exults that they've
'got you taped; you're in the play'. A couple quick asides – 'Here's your ID
/ Ideal for identifying one and all' and 'Invest your life in the memory bank;
ours the interest and we thank you' – once again reveals the ambitious
wordplay (about Pilgrim's life) and relentless fluctuations that soak A Passion
Play. A temperamental movement then builds expertly into a gallant cycle of
foreboding coils (led by more saxophone, of course) before a downpour of
syncopation and woodwinds create madcap majesty.

A brief drum-roll activates another wicked refrain, with guitar and keyboard
counterpoints and launching a moderately regal section for Anderson to champion
'tak[ing] the prize for instant pleasure'. With strident riffs from Barre and Evan
(and subdued accompaniment from Hammond-Hammond), it effortlessly
transforms into a more candid rocker in which Anderson counsels that 'all of your

best friends' telephones / never cooled from the heat of your hand'. A former theme reappears temporarily; from there, a freeform break exposes a residual section from the Château d'Hérouville tapes: 'Critique Oblique'.

A sinister ascension of textures takes over, as Anderson ensnares, 'Lover of the black and white / It's your first night / The Passion Play goes all the way / spoils your insides'. This decree is cut-off by two unexpected diversions – a spoken-word lashing about 'your little sister's immaculate virginity' and a sophomoric chant about how 'the examining body examined her body' – as well as more highly dynamic and theatrical accusations. Evan hurriedly recalls the 'memory bank' phrase in the midst of the sonic bombast, too, eventually leading to Anderson's folky reversal ('All of this and some of that's / the only way to skin the cat'). It's here that Hammond-Hammond proves the unsung hero since his behind-the-scenes contributions are outstanding.

Dizzying and miraculously synchronised classical/jazz freneticism and a conclusive fill from Barlow signal Anderson and Evan's quiet reprise to the 'Fulham Road' melody. In essence, the curtains have been drawn on the first half of A Passion Play; all that's left is for the tranquil and fantastical acoustic guitar, flute and synthesiser, and a final percussive collapse of 'Forest Dance #1' to bridge the gap between Pilgrim's voyage and the charming intermezzo quest of a formerly bespectacled rabbit.

'The Story of the Hare Who Lost His Spectacles' (Anderson, Hammond-Hammond, Evan)

Barlow and Evan's frisky exclamation at the end of 'Forest Dance #1' announces Hammond-Hammond's initial tongue-in-cheek declaration (which humorously ends with a vocal break and sniff). A frolicsome arrangement comprised of glockenspiel, piano, strings, horns, and other orchestral timbres escorts his narration until its resolution. It maintains its main melody from start to finish (via alternating instruments) with a variety of accompanying textures appearing, disappearing, and reappearing. What's most noticeable, then, is how these elements alter *around* that focal point and Hammond-Hammond's recital (which features tongue rolls and alliteration throughout, adding to the sense of childlike wonder). For instance, woodwinds, piano, and saxophone mix suspense and serenity when he introduces the characters; likewise, there's a menacing insert to foil Owl's 'scowling' and an elegant collapse (including organ) after Kangaroo shouts, 'I can't send Hare in search of anything'. Perhaps its most striking segment comes at the end when an overflow of heavenly strings and piano (beautifying a confession that 'Hare didn't care' about 'all of their tempting ideas') is violently juxtaposed by in-your-face insolence because 'the lost spectacles were his own affair'. After that, a quick classical postscript brings about the slightly revised 'Forest Dance #2' and the finale of Pilgrim's crossing. Even if its ludicrousness makes it feel out of place (given the serious nature of what bookends it), 'The Story of the Hare Who Lost His Spectacles' deserves praise for its levity and exceptional instrumentation.

'A Passion Play Part Two' (Anderson)

In general, the second part of *A Passion Play* – starting with the penultimate act, 'The Business Office of G. Oddie & Son (Two Days Later)' – is even more enchantingly traumatic and tricky. Anderson instantly paints a grief-stricken picture of loneliness and age as he sings, 'Old gentleman talk of when they were young / Of ladies lost, of erring songs' alongside acoustic guitar arpeggios, organ chirps, and rhythmic guidance. Together, they produce an imposing air of hopelessness that's cleverly set away for a sleeker digression about how 'the last hymn is sung and the devil cries, "More!"'.

An entrancing jam commences, led by saxophone and complemented by electric guitar, animated percussion, and rambunctious bass lines. Barlow's tremendous fill produces a unified retaliation and complex give-and-take before a melodramatic keyboard solo is transiently interrupted by a saintly countermelody and cries of 'La-la!' as if angels are watching Pilgrim's conflict. It's a utopic composition that subsequently allows for a lone organ bridge to herald Anderson's dirge ('Well, I'm all for leaving and that being done / I've put in a request to take up my turn').

Here, he seamlessly transitions into a fresh acoustic movement ('Where no-one has nothing and nothing is / Well-meaning fool'). It's a tactic he'll do again in 'Baker Street Muse' a couple of years later and it adds even more dejected magnificence to the mix. It also contrasts well the ensuing passage, in which he affirms, 'Summoned by name / I am the overseer over you' alongside a terrifically unusual aural triumph that's decked by low vocal exhales and echoes). This evolves into an uproariously peculiar party that finds him assuredly asserting, 'Fell with mine angels from a far better place / Offering services for the saving of face'. Unexpectedly, a severely stilted yet madcap disruption – and another call of 'Overseer!' – leaks into a seductive array of textures that are held together by Barlow's gripping syncopation. Horns modify the 'Passionate play / Joined round the maypole and dance' melody before an ending descent queues Pilgrim's 'Flight from Lucifer' (and the fourth act, 'Magus Perdé's Drawing Room at Midnight').

Up to this point, A Passion Play has presented some truly beguiling paths, but this section is likely the single catchiest route Jethro Tull has ever taken. Following some theistic organ chords, Anderson mixes reflections victoriously ('Here's the everlasting rub / Neither am I good or bad / I'd give up my halo for a horn / And the horn for the hat I once had') and delicate disclosures ('I thank everybody for making me welcome / I'd stay but my wings have just dropped off'). In-between, an even more tempting, strange, and erratic section takes over, showcasing a dynamic trade-off between stylish saxophone annotations, corrosive electric guitar, and flute. It's out-and-out irresistible.

Explosions lead into a soft and contemplative stream of acoustic guitar strokes, drums, and strings before Barre's fiery licks and Hammond-Hammond's bouncy bass prompts woodwinds and percussion to enter the fray. Anderson confidently directs 'Magus Perdé' to 'Take your hand from off the chain / Loose a wish to still the rain / The storm about to BE' prior to two asides: an impatient call to 'Break the circle / Stretch the lines / Call upon the devil' and a hipper, almost funky pronouncement about 'The passengers upon the ferry crossing / Waiting to be born' , with guitar aiding Anderson's cool dominance. A jovial jumble of ideas is placed side-by-side until Barre's whips punctuate jazzy spurts, probably the most unabashed showmanship on the LP.

Naturally, it returns home to continue Pilgrim's concluding notes and reincarnation ('Here am I / Roll the stone away / From the dark into ever-day!'). Anderson's epilogue once again reminds us that 'There was a rush along the Fulham Road / Into the ever-Passion Play' (much like he brought Thick as a Brick full circle upon completion, too). An extra bit of brazen orchestral oddness (and yelps of 'Steve! Caroline!' that connect to journalists Steve Peacock and Caroline Coon) helps *A Passion Play* fade away, cementing its place as Jethro Tull's greatest achievement (and therefore, one of the most criminally misjudged and underappreciated albums in progressive rock history).

Bonuses
Luckily, the 'An Extended Performance' release contains a lot more than its *Thick as a Brick* counterpart. For starters, the 'Foot of our Stairs' part reinserts a couple of lost verses (which, admittedly, don't sound quite as crisp as the rest of it, but that's to be expected). In addition, there are various mixes of both *A Passion Play* and *The Château d'Hérouville Sessions*, plus video clips of 'The Story of the Hare Who Lost His Spectacles' and the intro and outro footage used on the 1973 tour. It's a pertinent package, no doubt.

War Child (1974)

Personnel:
Ian Anderson: vocals, acoustic guitar, flute, alto, soprano, and sopranino saxophones
Martin Barre: electric and Spanish guitars
Barriemore Barlow: drums, glockenspiel, marimba, sundry percussion device
Jeffrey Hammond-Hammond: bass guitar, string bass
John Evan: piano, organ, synthesizer, piano accordion
Dee Palmer: orchestral arrangements
Robin Black: engineer
Produced at Morgan Studios, London, December 1973 – February 1974 by Ian Anderson and Terry Ellis
UK and US release date: October 1974.
Highest chart places: UK: 14, USA: 2
Running time: 39:21
Current edition: Chrysalis 2014 two-CD/two-DVD '40ᵗʰ Anniversary Theatre Edition' (Steven Wilson Remixed)

Seeing as how *A Passion Play*'s widely perceived inaccessibility made it a combative effort (to put it mildly), it makes sense that Jethro Tull veered toward 'shorter songs with more traditional shape and form' that were 'oriented to an onstage situation' with *War Child*. Focused around Dee Palmer's imperial orchestral treatments and fanciful, warm, and exuberant music, it mostly conveys a luscious and relaxed vibe (in the midst of tackling some deep topics). In that sense, its formula is best considered as a precursor to 1975's much stronger *Minstrel in the Gallery* rather than as a relatively underwhelming follow-up to the band's past four 1970s classics. Either way, *War Child* is certainly an important and valuable album whose simpler and more welcoming aesthetic aptly responded to the criticisms of its immediate progenitor and set the course for consequent greatness.

Originally, Anderson wanted to maintain Jethro Tull's expanded creative trajectory by making *War Child* a double LP (an orchestral soundtrack and a proper rock music collection) and black comedy film (not unlike Steven Wilson's initial idea for Porcupine Tree's 2005 darling, Deadwing). The latter – *War Child: A Musical Fantasy* – would've shared commonalities with *A Passion Play* in that it revolved around a teenager named Emily who gets caught up in a conflict between God (G. Oddie) and Satan (Samuel Luscious Browne) after being tricked by a guide named Peter Du Jour. At a January 1974 press conference held at the Eurohotel in Montreux, Switzerland, Anderson compared the feature-length movie to *Alice in Wonderland*, adding that it's about 'the way this girl copes with what she sees and hears and gets involved in'. Ideally, it would've been directed by Bryan Forbes and had the participation of actors John Cleese (as a 'humour consultant'), Sir Frederick Ashton, Donald Pleasance, and Leonard Rossiter, as well as choreographer Margot

Fonteyn and the face of *A Passion Play*, ballerina Jane Eve. Because 'there was simply no funding to be had through the UK film industry', Anderson and Terry Ellis looked to America. Unfortunately, though, they demanded an American director and cast, so Anderson ultimately decided to move on. Now, he appreciates the fact that such an off-the-wall film would never have been commercially successful anyway (although it might have done well with the arthouse crowd at festivals).

As for the soundtrack (which was to feature every member of the band as 'soloists within the orchestra framework'), about thirty minutes of it was produced despite not having a movie to accompany. Specifically, and with help from Palmer, Anderson's compositions included 'Field Dance', 'Waltz of the Angels', 'The Beach', 'War Child Theme', and a classical take on War Child's penultimate track, 'The Third Hoorah'. (Barre also contributed an acoustic guitar piece called 'Mime Sequence'). While shelved for decades after being recorded, snippets were used during the start and end of the group's mid-'70s concerts.

With two-thirds of the *War Child* trifecta fallen by the wayside, Jethro Tull decided to focus fully on the last component: a traditional studio album. That process was relatively easy and relaxing since some of it consisted of earlier material. Aside from the reworked Château d'Hérouville leftovers ('Skating Away on the Thin Ice of The New Day,' 'Bungle in the Jungle,' and 'Only Solitaire'), closer 'Two Fingers' derived from an abandoned song from the Aqualung sessions called 'Lick Your Fingers Clean'. Likewise, several songs – 'Saturation', 'Paradise Steakhouse', 'Good Godmother', and 'Tomorrow Was Today' – were recorded for *War Child* but left off because they 'either didn't fit the context ... or they were somehow flawed'.

Of that context, Anderson told Circus magazine in 1974 that yes, *War Child* isn't singularly conceptual, but its overarching theme is 'that all of us have a very aggressive instinct, which is something we're occasionally able to use for the betterment of ourselves. At other times, aggression at its worst is used as a very destructive element. When it's not at its worst, it remains merely comical'. Sonically, it once again found him toying with various saxophones, and while Palmer's arrangements effectively embellished the quintet's spirit throughout War Child, Anderson retrospectively finds them 'dense' and 'overwhelming' to a fault, especially in the quadrophonic version (a first for a Jethro Tull release).

The front cover of *War Child* – showcasing a negative image of Anderson in his 'minstrel' outfit superimposed over the skyline of Melbourne, Australia – has been interpreted as capturing his 'identification with the typical sarcastic, social commenting fools of Shakespeare's plays' and 'allud[ing] to telling references in songs such as "Only Solitaire"'. In contrast, the back cover integrates 'band members, wives, girlfriends, record company executives and photographic agency models, each depicting one of the songs on the album'. Interestingly, though, they were abstracted in reverse 'to somehow recreate

49

the feel' of *This Was*. Looking back, Anderson calls the end result 'an awful
pantomime ... [that's] very messy', yet for many fans, it stands as one of the
Jethro Tull's most iconic artworks.

Somewhat predictably (given their almost undivided ire toward *A Passion
Play*'s ostentatious scope), the press mostly praised War Child's return to form.
Forty-five years on, only a minority of devotees would place it as one of their
favourite Jethro Tull outings (even Anderson ranks it as decent 'designer pop-
rock' at best and cautions listeners to 'remember where [it] lay in the scheme
of things [within] that post-prog era'). Nevertheless, it's a reliably pleasing
entry that found them acclimating to the expectations of the epoch and laying
the groundwork for an improved Gallery eleven months later.

'War Child' (Anderson)
In an interview within the '40th Anniversary Theatre Edition,' Anderson reflects
that his initial description about the opening title track – 'It's ostensibly a love
song but not really a love song' about 'aggression and competitiveness' – isn't
quite right. Instead, he clarifies, 'I was definitely thinking about a child within a
conflict zone'. This revised account makes more sense given the first moments:
a collage of emergency sirens, gunfire, and bomb drops merging with domestic
life as a wife (whom Anderson calls 'Jackie ... the tea-lady at Morgan Studios')
asks her husband if he wants another cup. For sure, it founds a meek yet
gloomy reality to humanise that setting.

In a sense, this backdrop, coupled with the romantically pensive horns,
hums, and piano that arise from it, make 'War Child' feel like a direct ancestor
to Pink Floyd's The Wall. Before too long, Barlow, Barre, and Hammond-
Hammond chime in with tiptoeing advancement as Anderson cleanly promises
to take the listener 'down to that bright city mile' so they can 'show all of the
pleasures and none of the pain' (presumably associated with the neighbouring
urban destruction). The chorus heightens this sinister playfulness with livelier
guitar riffs, percussion, and saxophone romps. It's macabrely carnivalistic yet
appealingly anthemic, with Evan decorating each moment stylishly alongside
strings (that mimic the verses) and additional wartime sound effects. Like much
of the album, 'War Child' succeeds more for its crafty production and lavish
score than its fundamental songwriting, but it's still a winning way to start.

'Queen and Country' (Anderson)
This one continues the rowdy splendour of 'War Child' with an emphasis on
Evan's piano accordion. Melodically, it's a sensibly straightforward critique
of high society that's 'rooted in that rather buccaneering spirit and romantic
historical notion of going into the world to find things of beauty and desire
and commercial application'. Told via an account of seemingly proud sailors
who 'signed [their] souls away' half a decade ago, it catches Anderson inducing
the staunch grit of his *Benefit* days. Apart from that and Barre's biting double-
tracked solo, it's a satiating but marginally simplistic and repetitive selection.

'Ladies' (Anderson)

Miscellaneous chatter in a brothel begins this honourable 'lyric about ladies of the night' that came from Anderson wanting to 'put the veneer of respect on something that historically was a sordid profession'. Its oppressed acoustic guitar finger-picking and gratified woodwinds establish a dignified atmosphere that's soon ornamented by hand claps, sleigh bells, cymbals, and horns as Anderson layers his falsetto counterpoints during the chorus. Palmer adds heartening orchestration during the second half to bring more voluptuous esteem to the 'ladies who bless ... their heroes, [the] solitary soldiers', and Evan steers a sudden 1950s rock and roll breakdown as it ends. All in all, it's a lovely change of pace that hints at the mid-section style of *Minstrel in the Gallery*.

'Back-Door Angels' (Anderson)

As the title suggests, this one also has that 'Florence Nightingale with nice tits, short skirt and sexy legs kind of thing going on'. Whereas the previous tune was reasonably humble but regal, however, 'Back-Door Angels' is more multifaceted and morose, with Barlow's light taps supervising Anderson's forlorn flutes and verses. Meanwhile, Barre chimes in with some crunchy strikes, Hammond-Hammond trudges along agreeably, and Evan augments with some synthesiser and piano inflections. It's the ways in which these tones bounce off of each other that keeps the composition fresh and mesmerising, as the fivesome then dive into one of the most exhilarating jams on the LP. Naturally, Barre emblematically commands with classy roughness as horns, bass, and keyboards add skilful provocation. Each disposition is repeated again before acoustic guitar chords give birth to Anderson's final echoed solo remarks. Overall, it's a riveting and fertile number, and one of its last admissions – 'Think I'll sit down and invent some fool; some Grand Court Jester' – is possibly a slice of meta-commentary in that Anderson is commenting on his *War Child* costume (if not also foreshadowing his *Minstrel*).

'Sea Lion' (Anderson)

The first of several animal-oriented tracks on *War Child* – and thus, the first to hearken back to the Château d'Hérouville period, at least conceptually – the titular creature represents both 'a barometer of health' (relating to Anderson's upbringing near the sewage-infested shore of Blackpool) and 'the rather showbizzy, glossy world of animals ... being seemingly willing participants in entertaining people'. It contains two Anderson idiosyncrasies: an opening countdown and a spoken word deviation; plus, it slightly harkens back to the blues-rock scorch of the *Stand Up* era (intermixed with their newfound progressive rock darkness, Palmer's classical garlands, and some circus-esque surfaces within a waltz). Its full-bodied system is amazingly cultured, speckled, and invigorating, and its closing self-aware nod – 'It's the same old story to this Passion Play' – is satisfyingly sly.

'Skating Away on the Thin Ice of the New Day' (Anderson)

Beginning with Anderson humming the chorus as he pours a drink (perhaps tea, for a subtle link to the start of 'War Child'), 'Skating Away on the Thin Ice of the New Day' primarily conjures the yearning of 'Wond'ring Aloud' in its preliminary warm arpeggios and soft singing (although it's a bit more energetic). In contrast to the personal essence of that ballad, this one's stimulus – joint optimism after enduring 'a new mini-Ice Age resulting from global cooling' – is entirely universal. Lyrically, there's an overarching sense of existential autonomy throughout it ('Meanwhile, back in the Year One / When you belonged to no one' and 'Or, that everybody's on the stage / And it seems that you're the only person sitting in the audience,' for example, as well as another reference to 'the Passion Play'). Happily, his multi-layered vocals are enhanced by torrents of merry touches (such as electric guitar, flutes, piano accordion, glockenspiel, marimba, and miscellaneous percussive tools) to yield rejoiceful briskness that's downright delightful.

'Bungle in the Jungle' (Anderson)

This seventh inclusion is surely the most popular one on *War Child*, if not in their whole discography, and it's clear why. It continues the animal personification theme of the Château d'Hérouville sessions from the jump, as lion roars and human whistles support Barlow's unassuming beat around Anderson and Barre's prettily unified motif. Henceforth, it's a fairly characteristic arrangement with a picturesque mid-section (comprised of strings, woodwinds, and stacked acoustic guitar laments) and a chorus that's ripe for sing-alongs and radio airplay (which, ironically, is now 'too damn catchy for [Anderson's] own good'). In fact, it was successfully written to be a mainstream hit, reaching #12 in the U.S. charts and marking the last time Jethro Tull would ever crack the Top 40. By no means their most difficult undertaking, it's an amusing novelty if nothing else, and contrary to the misconception, it's wholly unrelated to the 1974 'Rumble in the Jungle' boxing match between Muhammad Ali and George Foreman.

'Only Solitaire' (Anderson)

Another holdover from France, 'Only Solitaire' permits Anderson to lambast the press (in particular, *Sounds* writer Steve Peacock), explaining that he creates music for himself and not for them. Distributed via plaintive reverberations and spunky acoustic trappings, shrewdly worded digs like 'The critics falling over to tell themselves he's boring ... Well, who the hell can he be when he's never had V.D. and doesn't even sit on toilet seats?' Take an authorised tangent mid-verse (another trademark) and halfway in. These days, Anderson might find it 'show[ing] weakness' as 'a childish riposte to negative criticism', but there's no denying how well it displays his aptitude for gloriously witty retribution.

'The Third Hoorah' (Anderson)

A breezy blend of bass taps, flutes, electric guitar patterns, and resolute drumming boosts this 'slightly more Scottish and folky' tribute to 'The Pirates of Penzance' (a tune Anderson, Evan, and Hammond-Hammond used to hear while at Blackpool Grammar). Correctly, then, it carries a strong-willed 'Three Musketeers going into battle' personality, with Evan using multiple timbres to teeter around perennial rhythmic vacillations and Anderson's ceremonial calls of 'War Child / Dance the days and nights away'. Right when it's becoming a tad monotonous, a speedy gush of strings, horns, and other orchestral rudiments – as well as bagpipes performed by 'a young busker ... and two of his mates' whom Anderson saw playing near the Chrysalis offices – join the band to bargain a wonderfully suitable yet imaginative interval. Accordingly, it's another case of an adequate song being elevated by its stupendous instrumentation (attributed in part to 'Beethoven's third and seventh symphonies').

'Two Fingers' (Anderson)

'The only track on the album that has got a heaven and hell sort of scenario', as Anderson specifies, 'Two Fingers' appropriately evokes the rock'n'roll zeitgeist of 1971 (namely, The Rolling Stones and The Who). In addition to that foundation, Evan's piano accordion flourishes permeate eccentrically among Anderson's saxophone outcries and driving melodies. It's also peppered with his penetrating theological derisions from the start – 'I'll see you at the weighing-in / When your life's sum-total's made / And you set your wealth in goodly deeds / Against the sins you've laid' – to close *War Child* on a wisp of mocking scrutiny.

Bonuses

The '40th Anniversary Theatre Edition' houses the anticipated accessories (stereo, 5.1 surround, and even quadrophonic mixes, as well as video clips of the Montreux photo session/press conference and promo footage for 'The Third Hoorah'). The real gem, however, is 'The Second Act', a compilation of the aforementioned associated recordings and soundtrack excerpts. 'Sea Lion II', 'The Orchestral War Child Theme', and 'War Child II' are obvious standouts for continuity alone, whereas the *Fahrenheit 451*-influenced 'Saturation' is a fierce treat, 'Quartet' is an uncanny and dissonant instrumental, and 'March, the Mad Scientist' is a passing acoustic ode Anderson says wouldn't exist without artists like Roy Harper. There's sufficiently more here as well, making this perhaps the biggest bang for your buck yet in terms of comprehensive Jethro Tull commemorations.

Minstrel in the Gallery (1975)

Personnel:
Ian Anderson: vocals, acoustic guitar, flute
Martin Barre: electric guitar
Barriemore Barlow: drums, percussion
Jeffrey Hammond-Hammond: bass guitar, string bass
John Evan: piano, organ
Dee Palmer: string quartet arrangements and conducting
Robin Black: engineer
Brian Ward: photography
Ron Kriss and J.E. Garnett – album artwork
Produced at Maison Rouge Mobile Studio, Monaco, May 1975 – June 1975 by Ian Anderson
UK and US release date: September 1975.
Highest chart places: UK: 20, USA: 7
Running time: 45:11
Current edition: Chrysalis 2015 two-CD/two-DVD '40th Anniversary: La Grande Édition' (Steven Wilson Remixed)

Even though 1974's *War Child* was a generally fruitful shot at returning to standard structures (albeit within the context of gorgeous symphonies and Anderson's token quirky appendages), its songwriting and level of ambition were a little lacklustre and regressive. In that way, it fits in as Jethro Tull's *Beatles for Sale*, whereas its heir (chronologically and, to some degree, methodically), *Minstrel in the Gallery*, comes across as 'a medieval Sgt. Pepper's' that bears comparison to peers like 'Fairport Convention, Renaissance, and Steeleye Span' (as Will Romano gauges). A significantly autobiographical work, it pulls together the baroque enrichments of *War Child*, the infectiously epic and convivial intricacy of *Thick as a Brick*, and the dynamic divergences of *Aqualung* (Anderson even says that the two 'share a bond') to cultivate one of their most ambitious and indispensable releases.

As *PopMatters'* Sean Murphy writes in 'Reappraising Ian Anderson's *Minstrel in the Gallery*', Jethro Tull 'were the kings of the hill in terms of consistency and quality' by 1975. Their tours were more successful and elaborate than ever before, including a sold-out five-night stint in February 2015, at the 20,000-seater Los Angeles Forum in America. Still, they had to be cautious of how British tax rates would impact their recording budget, leading them to seek possibilities once again abroad. Inspired by how much freedom The Rolling Stones had with their mobile studio (creatively and financially), Anderson commissioned Morgan Studios engineer Pete Smith (under the guidance of Robin Black) to build the Maison Rouge ('Red House'). Once finished, they chose to drive 'the 8-ton Mercedes truck' to the French Riviera to work on *Minstrel in the Gallery* within Radio Monte Carlo.

In spite of those conveniences – as well as the draw of 'impromptu badminton games' and 'local beach ... temptations' – the making of *Minstrel in the Gallery* wasn't entirely fun. Truthfully, 'such distractions and other personal problems within the band meant that it was not functioning as well ... as it had on previous albums', leaving Anderson to somewhat begrudgingly 'take more of a prominent and introspective role'. In later years, he would admit to 'being a bit too hard on them' because he was 'as bad as they were, really'. Beyond those recreational deterrents, though, Anderson recalls 'something lacking in terms of the group's empathy as a musical outfit' in conjunction with 'internal frictions'. Hammond-Hammond (who officially left Jethro Tull – and music as a whole – at the end of 1975, but we'll get to that later) concurs, adding that the quintet had been acting like 'a wandering bunch of minstrels'. In contrast, Barre and Barlow now see the situation as justified and logical, if also arduous and incongruous.

Providentially, the resulting music was unquestionably worth the background hardships. A towering merger of complicated communal forces and 'singer-songwriter-with-acoustic-guitar wavelengths', it found Anderson and Palmer working on material concurrently (compared to how either the songs or classical arrangements were written first on previous LPs). Originally, they 'envisaged using a full orchestra to accompany the band'; yet, those initial sessions with a local ensemble 'proved disastrous' because they 'struggled to keep time with the unfamiliar rock music'. Ultimately, they veered toward 'some old friends' (including violinist Patrick Halling, who played on *War Child*, and the all-girl string quartet currently touring with Jethro Tull). Anderson comments that 'the strings ... work better than on any other album [they've] made', and while that's a debatable prospect, they certainly meld with Anderson's exceptional songwriting more innately than on *War Child*.

Capturing 'the wizened perspective of an adult who has toured the world [and] seen some things', *Minstrel in the Gallery* finds Anderson wrestling with 'loves, lusts, pains, regrets, shortcomings, and beliefs' regarding self-actualisation and other existential quandaries related to his recent divorce from Jennie Franks, his continuing disgruntlement with the musical press, and the burdens of creating and touring, among other subjects. Rather than relate to a fictionalised account, the title of the sequence could be seen as representing Anderson's self-image amidst all of the surrounding turmoil.

The artwork of *Minstrel in the Gallery* does a fine job visually conveying the essence of its music. Its front cover was based on a 19th century print by Joseph Nash titled 'Twelfth Night Revels in the Great Hall, Haddon Hall, Derbyshire' and its back cover simply shows the band looking over the main hall of the Radio Monte Carlo studio gallery. As with *War Child*, they didn't know which image would go where until 'the last minute', and Anderson 'wanted to avoid it being too twee and historical' while remaining 'punchy and cogent'. Few would argue that the end result doesn't satisfy all of those prerequisites, but he still finds it among 'the worst Jethro Tull album covers ever' because of how busy and sprawling it is.

Minstrel in the Gallery received Gold Certification in both America and the UK, and while journalists at the time were still divided on it overall, *Melody Maker*'s Harry Docherty declared it 'the most important album [they] have made in three years'. Fascinatingly, *The Guardian*'s Robin Denslow – alongside several other writers – viewed it as a 'low-key' solo album, to which the players strongly disagree. Barre, for example, concedes that Anderson's private irritations and need to 'work all of the time instead of partak[ing] in leisure activities' led to his 'musical writing peak' across some lone acoustic tracks. Similarly, Anderson says that his growing confidence as a guitarist is partially to blame, as is his tendency to sit 'alone in the studio' while the other guys were elsewhere. That said, he was 'wholeheartedly' trying to get the other four musicians involved.

Despite the interpersonal (and personal) tensions that occurred during its development, *Minstrel in the Gallery* radiates poised and cohesive variability. By mixing together all of their present personas into an all-encompassing aural entrée, Jethro Tull offered something for every fan without sacrificing excellence in any category. As such, it's undoubtedly a crucial moment in their catalogue and an ageless candidate for graceful musings.

'Minstrel in the Gallery' (Anderson, Barre)

Aqualung saw Jethro Tull instituting its knack for kicking things off with a sweeping title track, and *Minstrel in the Gallery* ranks right alongside it (as will *Songs from the Wood* in 1977). Written 'from a personal point of view of being onstage [and] looking out at an audience' (or from the perspective of Anderson creating in the mezzanine gallery that overlooked the main hall of Radio Monte Carlo), it instantly sets a noble scene as Palmer announces 'strolling players' for his 'lord and lady' within Anderson's spoken reaction and lone handclaps. Afterwards, his stately acoustic guitar strums, flute complements, foot stomps, and stern yet frisky verses (consisting of erudite repartee like 'He polarised the pumpkin-eaters / Static-humming panel-beaters / Freshly day-glowed factory cheaters') make for an inviting and electrifying narrative set-up.

Of course, Barre then unleashes one of his most career-defining performances: a hodgepodge of hypnotically intermittent riffs (that were 'partly improvised, partly formalised [from] a guitar solo that he'd been doing on stage') backed with faultless twist-and-turn resourcefulness by Barlow and Hammond-Hammond. It's easily one of the band's most irresistibly valiant and dexterous passages ever, and it's capped off with ingeniously discreet syncopation before everyone settles in unison on the next movement. Here, Anderson and Barre instrumentally play off of each other expertly before the former reprises and further explicates his opening account with more piercing heft and neighbouring depth (including organ wails). Finally, his gleeful ad-libs as the music concludes certify his enjoyment in completing one of Jethro Tull's most exemplary listens.

'Cold Wind to Valhalla' (Anderson)

Anderson's titular introduction makes this Norse mythology-inspired second selection immediately intimate. Specifically, it's built upon the 'huge afterlife hall of the slain, overseen by the god Odin, to which Valkyries took warrior heroes when they died'; fittingly, it's proclivity for downtrodden acoustic guitar and flute combinations – together with his woeful singing and Barlow's faint accents – portrays well the sentiment of how 'there aren't many ... modern type [courageous] heroes' left. Anderson paints a notably vivid and researched picture with lines such as 'Midnight lonely whisper cries / "We're getting a bit short on heroes lately" / Sword-snap fright-white pale goodbyes / In the desolation of Valhalla'. As you'd expect, 'Cold Wind to Valhalla' gets energised about halfway in, allowing Barre and Palmer to add some panicked highlights while everyone else upholds order. It's a thrillingly frigid piece from beginning to end.

'Black Satin Dancer' (Anderson)

An 'unashamed sexual bravado song', Black Satin Dancer' is cited by Barre as 'a stand out' from the set, and for good reason. At first, its spacious woodwind swirls, confrontational thumps from Hammond-Hammond, easy-going piano intervals, and restful vocals channel younger Jethro Tull; once the strings take off as Anderson sings, 'Thin wind whispering on broken mandolin', however, it feels suitably evolved and tasteful. Evan's constant sneaking adds a lot, too, as does the Zeppelin-esque combo of fresh percussive treats, plunging bass lines and bluesy electric guitar clamours. It calls back to the *Stand Up/Benefit* era afterwards when the arrangement pacifies and then speeds up as Anderson inhales in-between flute notes. By the end, its roughness takes it far away from where it started (well, until the closing recap), yet that only augments its exultantly brazen testimony.

'Requiem' (Anderson)

Comparing this to 'Wond'ring Aloud' is nearly unavoidable, but that doesn't take away from its sparse blissfulness. As one of the most romantic and beautiful elegies Anderson's ever penned, it's an utterly heavenly realisation of acoustic guitars, strings, and wistful harmonised remembrances (concerning the 'parting of the ways after the death of an affair, laying to rest the ghost of a failed relationship'). Although glimpses like 'Well, my lady told me, stay / I looked aside and walked away' and 'Saw her face in the tear-drop black cab window / Fading into the traffic. Watched her go' may seem pulled from his life, Anderson insists that it's a 'much more generalised' account of such heartache. Surprisingly, 'Requiem' was going to be 'much longer ... with more verses and an arrangement which included John Evan on piano playing a Bach-like descending progression'. Sadly (or perhaps fortunately), that 'proved difficult to record', so they took 'one more crack at it' with a different approach and the rest is history.

'One White Duck / 010 = Nothing at All' (Anderson)

Continuing the theme of the previous track, this one is a 'deliberate juxtaposition' between a 'slightly naff, cosy, cuddly, lovey-dovey world' and a 'rather cynical, dark, vindictive breaking up of a relationship'. Really, it alludes to Anderson's separation from Franks by referencing the British notion that a married couple has their 'ducks in a row' (so a lone duck represents a single person). His vocal wavers add nostalgic fragility to his acoustic guitar outlines, detailing 'the cheesy fifties stereotypical lower middle-class family home environment with ... three china ducks on a wall'. The string quartet's faintly devastating attachments bring closure to his empowered tenderness ('And the motorway's stretching right out to us all / As I pull on my old wings; one white duck on your wall').

Conversely, the '010 = Nothing at All' portion (which 'owes something to [Anderson's] origins in blues and the more aggressive sixties folky lyrical stuff of the likes of Bob Dylan') is more antagonistically stark. There's a ricochet to his scornful deliveries ('But remember your way in is also my way out / And love's four-letter word is no compensation') and more aggression in his playing; likewise, Palmer's contributions have disappeared, aiding the harsh veracity of estrangement that comes once the splendours of love are silenced.

'Baker St. Muse' (Anderson)

Considering the poor reception of *A Passion Play*, few listeners would've anticipated *Minstrel in the Gallery* ending (well, just about) with a nearly seventeen-minute, 'four-part observation of the seedier side of [Anderson's] then home town of London'. In particular, he wrote it about his time in Marylebone in 1974, when he'd simply wander around the namesake 'taking in the sights and sounds'. Aptly, almost the entire suite emits sunny spectatorship during its superlative nonstop flow, making it a bite-sized offspring of *Thick as a Brick* that ceaselessly captivates.

Humorously and amiably, Anderson starts off by screwing up the maiden acoustic guitar motif (even mumbling, 'Shit, shit, shit, shit, shit' before trying again). Once he gets it right, its elegant erudition serves as a fine illustration of his aforementioned 'growing confidence' with the instrument. Equally, verses like 'Indian restaurants that curry my brain / Newspaper warriors changing the names / They advertise from the station stands / With cold print hands' radiate youthful appreciation for the surrounding culture above reserved yet heavenly classical addendums and piano chords. It's a divine concoction that's delightfully intensified after the chorus, when Barre, Hammond-Hammond, and Barlow burst in with mirrored fervour before punching up another verse to be even more intoxicating. A brief jam follows that pits Barre's sharp realities against Anderson's poetic dreams as the rest of the rhythm section grooves along. Subsequently, Anderson offers a feisty curve ('Walking down the gutter, thinking, "How the hell am I today?"') and Barre takes over with breathtaking multitracked mastery.

A cathartic acoustic deviation bleeds into the next chapter, 'Pig-Me and the Whore', in which Anderson's quick wordplay – 'Testicle testing / Wallet ever-bulging / Dressed to the left, divulging' – is engrossingly jubilant and peppered with nuances from the other musicians. His voice then pairs with strings to lead into the appropriately titled 'Nice Little Tune' instrumental; it's a gorgeously aerial meeting of Palmer and Jethro Tull's specialities that truly feels like a compromise between the friendly textures of Thick as a Brick and the trance-inducing intricacy of A Passion Play. The resulting 'Crash-Barrier Waltzer' changes course to be among the most hauntingly remorseful routes that the band's ever driven. The string quartet escorts Anderson's dejected strums and hammerings as he tells of 'drunken bums' and 'Some only son's mother / Baker Street casualty' with graceful, winding subjugation. It's awe-inspiringly sorrowful.

Sounds of traffic sneak beneath flute and acoustic guitar garnishes to segue into the finale, 'Mother England Reveries'. Even more dramatic and sullen that the former part, its violins, viola, and cello swell comfortingly around Anderson's thematic fingerpicking and sobering confessions (including one, 'I have no time for *Time Magazine* or *Rolling Stone*', that alludes to his real-life issues with music journalism). In a brilliantly understated move (that harkens back to the 'Well-meaning fool' switch in *A Passion Play*), it transforms mid-sweep into a more rousing direction – about 'a little boy stood on a burning log' – that brings the whole album full circle by having him declare, 'One day I'll be a minstrel in the gallery / and paint you a picture of the queen'). In this moment, the rest of the quintet comes in to expound Anderson's bucolic victory. As for the remaining couple of minutes, they're filled with eccentric reprisals of earlier ideas that shift with potent creativity and suddenness. Following a triumphant climax of drums, guitars, and piano, Anderson tries to leave the studio while singing, 'I'm just a Baker Street Muse' but then yells, 'I can't get out!', granting another snippet of comedy to another one of his supreme works.

'Grace' (Anderson)

The thirty-seven-second 'Grace' acts as an epilogue, with 'a carefully designed poignancy to it'. More precisely, its happy-go-lucky balminess comes across like a detached excerpt from 'One White Duck / 010 = Nothing at All', with Anderson greeting the sun, a bird, his breakfast, and his lady before asking, 'May I buy you again tomorrow?' So, it can be seen as 'a simple expression of giving thanks' that also houses 'a degree of cynicism, and [Anderson] saying that nothing in life is for free. We have to put back in what we take out'. Either way, it's a pretty little piece to wrap up *Minstrel in the Gallery*'s grateful aesthetic.

Bonuses

Like the *War Child* update, the '40th Anniversary: La Grande Édition' proffers stereo, 5.1 surround, and quadrophonic mixes of the album and associated recordings (which basically means 'Summerday Sands', an orchestral and acoustic – but still hefty – B-side to 'Minstrel in the Gallery' that concerns 'two lovers on the sand'). Outside of that, a promo clip, and some alternate takes of 'Grace', 'One White Duck', and 'Requiem', the true treasure is Jakko Jakszyk's stereo and 5.1 surround remixes of the 'Live at the Palais des Sports, Paris, 5th July 1975' concert. As you might expect, it showcases Jethro Tull at the peak of their powers and is a must-see for aficionados.

Too Old to Rock 'n' Roll: Too Young to Die! (1976)

Personnel:
Ian Anderson: vocals, acoustic guitar, flute, harmonica, electric guitar, percussion
Martin Barre: electric guitar
Barriemore Barlow: drums, percussion
John Glascock: bass guitar, backing vocals
John Evan: piano, organ
Dee Palmer: orchestral arrangements, saxophone (5), piano (11)
Maddy Prior: backing vocals (8)
Angela Allen: backing vocals (2, 7)
Robin Black: engineer
Michael Farrell and David Gibbons: cover design and illustrations
Produced at Maison Rouge Mobile Studio, Monaco (except 'Too Old to Rock 'n' Roll: Too Young to Die' and 'The Chequered Flag (Dead or Alive)', which were recorded at Morgan Studios in Brussels), November 1975 – January 1976 by Ian Anderson
UK release date: April 1976. US release date: May 1976.
Highest chart places: UK: 25, USA: 14
Running time: 42:26
Current edition: Chrysalis 2015 two-CD/two-DVD 'TV Special Edition' (Steven Wilson Remixed)

Up until *War Child*, Jethro Tull had been on an unwavering ascension in terms of artistic valour and innovation; while that seventh studio outing was still quite good – as discussed earlier in this book – it marked a dip in both areas, which is why *Minstrel in the Gallery*'s creative luxuries were so rewarding. Inevitably, the band's ninth effort would have a lot to live up to, and despite some adequately fetching moments scattered throughout its thoroughly familiar formula, 1976's *Too Old to Rock and Roll: Too Young to Die!* falls short in every respect (even Barre admits that 'it didn't have the same impact'). To put it bluntly, it's unexpectedly perfunctory and inconsequential, solidifying the inconsistent nature of Jethro Tull's mid-1970s output. Beyond that, it stands as their weakest attempt of the whole decade (which is just as much the fault of its own quality as it is a testament to the prodigious works that surround it).

While not an overt detriment to the LP, the parting of Hammond-Hammond, who 'always thought of [himself] as the non-musician in the band' in November 1975 – following an extensive tour, although he'd first announced his plans before *Minstrel in the Gallery* was recorded – marked the poignant end of an era. After all, he'd been there during Jethro Tull's most creatively fruitful period. Specifically, he left so that he could return to painting, now reflecting that it was 'the correct decision for everyone' because he knew that in the end, 'those friendships would endure, outliving the temporary sense of loss'. Anderson recollects trying to change his mind, whereas Barre 'admired'

61

him for listening to his intuition, adding, 'He earned his place in the band because he was a great showman and entertainer... [He's] a great person for whom I have nothing but love and respect'. By all admittances, then, it was a cordial goodbye, and naturally, there was inherent pressure on whoever took over bass duties. As Anderson reminisces, he'd already had John Glascock in 'the back of [his] mind' since sharing the stage with his former flamenco rock ensemble, Carmen, earlier that year. No doubt, Glascock (or Brittle Dick, as he'd affectionately come to be known) does the best he can with the overarchingly lacklustre material.

On that note, the concept of *Too Old to Rock and Roll: Too Young to Die!* certainly seems less ambitious in both formulation and execution than those of its predecessors. Conceived as a stage musical (starring Adam Faith) with 'the light humour and the warmth that wasn't on the preceding album', Anderson and Palmer eventually landed on a more conventional set of songs circling around 'an ageing and retired rock star named Ray Lomas as he wins money on a decadent quiz show' but then attempts suicide on his motorcycle because he feels disconnected from modern society. Fortunately, he only ends up in a coma before awakening to discover that 'society has changed again, and his style of dress and music are now popular'. Finally, he decides to 'become an overnight sensation' and idol for youthful fans. (Much of those details are only revealed in the comic strip accompanying the cover art.) Notwithstanding its deeper (and reportedly non-autobiographical link to Anderson's friction with the budding punk scene) message of how unpopular styles, fads, and the like will 'come back around' if the proprietors 'stick to it', this tale, like the music and songwriting it spawns, is serviceable but tame when likened to past benchmarks.

Those gripes incorporated, *Too Old to Rock and Roll: Too Young to Die!* is not a bad listen; it's just vastly underdeveloped (and thus, disappointing) in every way. Time and time again, Jethro Tull had aimed higher and gone farther, so while this sequence still pleases as it plays, it's ultimately trite and forgettable when measured against its siblings. In fact, Anderson now admits that it's 'not ... very satisfying', and at the time, almost all professional critics agreed. As for sales, it was the only new Jethro Tull album of the 1970s to not earn Gold certification. Thankfully, though, they would soon revitalise their style once again to forest a superior set of Songs.

'Quizz Kid' (Anderson)

To be fair, 'Quizz Kid' shines in its conceptual continuity – it begins with the touchingly misty-eyed first verse of the title track – and ability to allure with complex catchiness. The contrast between that delicate prelude (to be discussed in more depth soon) and the strident guitar riffs that introduce the song proper is cleverly jarring, and the complementary flutes, drums, and bass fit well. From there, Anderson strums and narrates excitedly as he views Lomas trying out for a quiz show that 'may be barbaric but it's fun'. Behind him, Glascock and Evan enchant with playfully funky ideas while Barre's muted tones, Barlow's relaxed backbone, and Palmer's campy horns add more carefree and hopeful sophistication to pertinently capture Lomas' optimistic and figurative roll of the dice. It's genuinely sweet to hear the band exude childlike exhilaration in the midst of maintaining *Minstrel*'s method.

'Crazed Institution' (Anderson)
A mostly rudimentary but pleasing jingle, it conjures The Who's *Tommy* in its exploration of first-time stardom ('Crawl inside your major triad / Curl up and laugh as your agent scores another front-page photograph'). Glascock's beatific harmonies suit Anderson's elated lead vocals nicely, and the instrumentation is filled with festive touches (especially piano and woodwinds) that pop in and out as it goes. At the same time, its surface level simplicity and repetition generate little more than an enjoyably throwaway means of advancing the plot.

'Salamander' (Anderson)
Intentionally or not, its core acoustic guitar work sounds like an alternate take of 'Cold Wind to Valhalla' (albeit with more Spanish flair). According to Anderson and Barre, its 'hybrid tuning' (not quite open but with 'a number of open strings which allows you to play things that you can't play with regular concert E tuning') makes it one of the most rewarding yet difficult pieces they arranged together. Furthermore, Anderson is filled with ethereal longing as he calls out to a girl 'born in the sun-kissed flame' who walks by his window 'in [a] Kensington haze', and the dual flute and guitar solo near the end adds a coat of intrigue. Best of all, its cryptic chill keeps it purposeful and arresting in the face of its habitual aura.

'Taxi Grab' (Anderson)
Barre's multitracked electric licks (together with inventive single-note counterpoints, harmonica interruptions, and closing harmonic plucks) give way to a bluesy rocker that, while certainly produced and performed well enough, is marred by mediocre songwriting and a tedious arrangement. True, some may view it as a throwback to Jethro Tull's late 1960s repertoire, but even that casts it in a poor light since *This Was* and *Stand Up* featured more go-getting and eye-catching compositions. Even by those standards, 'Taxi Grab' is discouragingly lazy and trivial.

'From a Dead Beat to an Old Greaser' (Anderson)
The intersecting low and high-pitched voices really bring out the emotion of this bleak acoustic trip down memory lane. Anderson bears defeat and compunction as he fills his befittingly modest melody with earnest recognitions like 'Old queers with young faces / Who remember your name / Though you're a dead beat with tired feet / Two ends that don't meet'. The minor percussion

and continuous orchestration add to its tear-jerking utopia – that is, until saxophone, bass, and heftier drumming fleetingly take command to scatter some vibrant spice on an otherwise gentle platter of refined heartbreak. All in all, it's an outstanding demonstration of garnering great despair out of a minimalistic diagram.

'Bad-Eyed and Loveless' (Anderson)
The shortest song on *Too Old to Rock and Roll: Too Young to Die!*, its tinge of American Southern rock (i.e., the Allman Brothers Band) gives its barren acoustic-guitar-with-vocals template a novel maleficence. Anderson has always done well at sounding a touch bullying, and he does so here in murmuring about a nameless woman – his Salamander, now rejecting him at a bar– who's 'a young man's fancy and an old man's dream' as she 'turns other women to envious green'. Although its sonic chill and emptiness adequately represents Lomas' loveless abandonment, one can't help but wish that there was more to it musically (even if it is only a hair past two minutes in length).

'Big Dipper' (Anderson)
Each instrument gradually piles on to yield a sumptuously organic starting point that recalls the DIY blues bustle of Jethro Tull's oldest tapes. Barre and Glascock steer with identical hipness while Barlow, Anderson, and Evan cavort around them with laidback composure (well, aside from their tricky chromatic climbs in-between the verses and chorus). On that end, Anderson – with backing support from Glascock –attractively projects Lomas' gladness as he thinks back to his youth at a theme park, riding the titular rollercoaster (in addition to 'Hanging out in the penny arcades / Shaking up the Tower Ballroom / Throwing up in the bathroom'). Like much of the album, it's definitely reductive in terms of its songwriting and score, but it also has an unchecked and communal spring in its step that's passably tempting.

'Too Old to Rock 'n' Roll: Too Young to Die!' (Anderson)
Bursting out with heroic and stylish melodrama (courtesy of another equal partnership between forthright playing and classical undertones), it promptly signifies the start of the story's wrap-up. The little segue into the above-mentioned misty-eyed verses is effective as well, giving Anderson a caring platform on which to lovingly reminiscence about how Lamas was 'unfashionable to the end' as he escapes his current situation via his motorcycle, Doris (only to crash and end up in the hospital). The track then becomes more boisterous (save for a saintly reversion near the end) thanks to variety show horns and strings, quick-witted syncopation, and dim piano and guitar foils. Overall, it's a bit corny and commercial (especially at the end, with the up-tempo jam), yet its incontestably appealing as a multifaceted celebration that requires at least some sing-along participation.

'Pied Piper' (Anderson)

Having awoken from a coma to find himself a 'Piped Piper' of fashion, Lomas relishes being admired and popular as he hands out 'his small cigars to the kids from school' and drives them around on Doris. It's an uplifting and halcyon – if mildly mawkish – resolution to Lomas' tribulations that's presented with endearing softness as an acoustic ballad with quaint add-ons (direct rhythms and a *Passion Play*-esque fusion of fairy-tale piano intervals, electric guitar arpeggios, and woodwind echoes).

'The Chequered Flag (Dead or Alive)' (Anderson)

There's a fantastical majesty to Evan's keyboard motif – aided by Barre and Palmer's calming adjuncts –that aids Anderson's reflective guardian angel codas. Before long, the rest of the band appears to add moving sturdiness and engaging variations to his bittersweet insights ('The still-born child can't feel the rain / As the chequered flag falls once again / The deaf composer completes his final score / He'll never hear the sweet encore'). From start to finish, it shines with terrific ambivalence, leaving the listener in amazement and ending a mostly unexceptional collection on its greatest note.

Bonuses

The 'TV Special Edition' of *Too Old to Rock and Roll: Too Young to Die!* personifies its television gimmick with the audio and video for its titular TV film (in DTS, DDS, and Dolby Digital 5.1), plus five original album tracks, a host of associated recordings (such as 'Salamander's Rag Time', 'Commercial Traveller', and 'Strip Cartoon'), and the flat transfer, quadrophonic, and 96/24 stereo PCM versions of the album. It's an impressive buffet of extras for those who hold the sequence in tall regard.

Songs from the Wood (1977)

Personnel:
Ian Anderson: vocals, acoustic guitar, flute, mandolin, whistles, cymbals, all instruments (2)
Martin Barre: electric guitar, lute, additional material
Barriemore Barlow: drums, tabor, nakers, glockenspiel, bells, marimba
John Glascock: bass guitar, backing vocals
John Evan: piano, organ, synthesizer
Dee Palmer: piano, synthesizer, portative pipe organ, saxophone, additional material
Robin Black: engineer
Thing Moss and Trevor White: assistant engineers
Keith Howard: woodcutter
Jay L. Lee: front cover painting
Shirt Sleeve Studio: back cover
Produced at Morgan Studios, London, September – November 1976 by Ian Anderson
UK and US release date: February 1977
Highest chart places: UK: 13, USA: 8
Running time: 41:17
Current edition: Chrysalis 2017 three-CD/two-DVD 40th Anniversary 'The Country Set' (Steven Wilson Remixed)

Too Old to Rock and Roll: Too Young to Die! was not a highpoint for Jethro Tull. It was cherishable at times, yes, but on the whole, its comparably lightweight bravura and content signalled a need to reach farther than that now-hackneyed strategy going forward. Luckily, the sextet felt that instinct, too, and decided on a new folk-rock direction that was stirred, in part, by 'British pagan folklore', as well as Anderson's recent appetite for 'countryside life' and various interactions with acts like Steeleye Span (for whom he produced 1974's *Now We Are Six*). Entwining 'traditional instruments and melodies with hard rock drums and electric guitars', 1977's *Songs from the Wood* – the first of a stylistic trio that resolved with 1978's *Heavy Horses* and 1979's *Stormwatch* – was exactly the impassioned and experimental breath of fresh air the troupe needed to reinvigorate their exclusive and beloved palette. Forty-odd years later, it remains a top-tier Jethro Tull release and a timeless beacon for the entire progressive folk subgenre.

Everyone involved with it embraced its renewed and pivotal pastoral magnificence, which is why an extra title line – 'with kitchen prose, gutter rhymes and divers' – appeared between the group and LP names, not to mention why UK adverts began by professing:

Jethro Tull present 'Songs from the Wood'. A new album of Old Magic. Songs from the Wood. It's inspired by the thought that perhaps nature isn't as gentle as we'd like to believe. And it takes as its theme the natural and supernatural inhabitants of the woodlands of old England. Warm and friendly, harsh and bitter by turns, it includes 'Ring Out Solstice Bells' as well as Tull's new single 'The Whistler' and seven other songs. Find a quiet spot and listen to it soon.

Made just after they'd finished touring *Too Old to Rock and Roll: Too Young to Die!* and returned to England, *Songs from the Wood* gave Anderson 'an opportunity to evaluate and reflect upon the cultural and historical significance of making [a] commitment to English residency... . [It's] a reaffirmation of our Britishness' (as he told Christopher Scapelliti in a September 1999 interview with Guitar World). Likewise, Martin Webb's liner notes for the 40th anniversary 'Country Set' find Anderson also crediting the book Folklore, Myths and Legends of Britain (given to him by manager Jo Lustig in 1976) for inspiring its sounds and themes: '[It] certainly gave me thoughts about the elements of characters and stories that played out in my songwriting ... which then carried on over to the *Heavy Horses* ... and *Stormwatch* album[s]'.

While Anderson was still leading the charge, he acknowledges that 'the band [namely, Barre and the now-official Palmer] had more to do with the elements of the songs' than on any other studio production. This gives Songs from the Wood a sort of 'band vibe' that'd been missing 'since This Was and Stand Up'. Aside from reminding him of his childhood, living in the country 'brought the guys in the group together'. Actually, he'd 'deliberately leave the studio and let them come up with some arrangements and ideas' in an attempt to 'add a social as well as musical identity'. That camaraderie sheens through nearly every entry here, making for a remarkably charming collection.

Romano claims that nothing else in the Jethro Tull catalogue 'matches the musical balance achieved with *Songs from the Wood*', and he's got a point. By mingling things like 'traditional folk odd tempos, church music in the counterpoint style of Giovanni Pierluigi Palestrina ... medieval minstrelsy, Renaissance dance tunes ... [and] Pagan imagery that speaks directly to the past', Jethro Tull fashioned a rehabilitated recipe that's soothingly learned, gregarious, and catchy. This daring fineness was rewarded critically, too, earning Jethro Tull a pillar of unanimous applause they hadn't seen in years. It was their last top ten record in America, with only one single, 'The Whistler', charting (at #59). In recent years, Rolling Stone championed it as perhaps 'the group's best record ever', PROG placed it at #76 in their list of 'The 100 Greatest Prog Albums of All Time', and many revered progressive rock persons favour it. Clearly, Songs from the Wood's nine cups of wonder still set fire to fans' hearts in the morning, afternoon, and at midnight, too.

'Songs from the Wood' (Anderson)
'Songs from the Wood', like 'Aqualung' and 'Minstrel in the Gallery' before it, is a tour-de-force titular launching point that parades Jethro Tull's updated

panache. Its idyllic preliminary verses ('Let me bring you songs from the wood / To make you feel much better than you could know') are superbly hospitable and exuberant as they find the band trying something new: interlocking vocal harmonies that originated centuries prior and were also revived with peers like Gentle Giant. Of course, the subsequent addition of spirited and fluctuating rural timbres – woodwinds, hand claps, acoustic guitars, whistles, bass, piano, and amused drumming – adds spellbinding scenic joviality.

Seamlessly, the music takes a more menacing path around the chorus, when Barre, Barlow, and Glascock unite in hasty dominance in-between Evan's pacifying organ blowouts. Next, Glasock follows his lead as cymbals crash and electric guitar riffs recoil with hypnotising irregularity before another choral chant gives way to an awesome flute solo. More incredibly intricate start-and-stop trickery proceeds until the opening simplicity and chaotic chorus come back around to offer ultimate bursts of tranquillity and trauma, respectively. It's a dashing cut of continuity that cements 'Songs from the Wood' as one of Jethro Tull's most joyfully challengingly, refreshing, and multi-layered configurations to date.

'Jack-in-the-Green' (Anderson)
Performed entirely by Anderson, this nod to the celebration of May Day contrasts the sophistication of its predecessor well by offering a humbler array of acoustic guitar zeal, periodic flute flourishes, bass and percussive accents, and reverberated and raw singing (a signature feature of the whole record). At first, Anderson's aggressive deliveries seems marginally incongruous to the pleasantries around it, but they soon feel at home as an essential method of delivering the immensely vivid and regretful tale about a man who 'drinks from the empty acorn cup / The dew that dawn sweetly bestows'. Beyond granting a momentary reprieve between two elaborate compositions, the track testifies to Anderson's dexterity and ingenuity as a lone artist (especially considering that he conceived it all at once one Sunday afternoon and recorded it in a few hours, with help from Black).

'Cup of Wonder' (Anderson)
The central woodwind/acoustic guitar refrain alone makes 'Cup of Wonder' infectiously life-affirming (and the complements by Barre, Barlow, and Glascock don't hurt, either). Continuing the May Day allusion of 'Jack-in-the-Green', its celebration of festive foods and communal fondness – 'Pass the plate to all who hunger / Pass the wit of ancient wisdom / Pass the cup of crimson wonder' – is so disarmingly sunny and organic that you fundamentally feel like you're a part of the party. A large part of that feat is Anderson's friendly demeanour (aided by occasional isolated angelic ascensions), plus its dizzying collage of rustic surfaces. The mid-section flamboyance – comprising a joined piano and electric guitar rendition of the refrain that melts into a rapturous floral jam –

is intoxicatingly resplendent. Like much of *Songs from the Wood*, it's nothing short of unbridled aural gaiety.

'Hunting Girl' (Anderson)

Evan's foreboding gothic organ primer – assisted by a mutably handsome dose of mischievous flutes, guitar and bass ambushes, and marching syncopation – provides a chilling milieu for Anderson's springy yet advisory storytelling. Throughout, the score lavishly chases his devilish cautions about 'this high-born Hunting Girl' who 'took this simple man's downfall in hand'; once again, there's an incessantly sublime exchange between established ideas and added novelties (including a trademark transitory duel between Barre and Anderson, as well as more charismatic backing voices) that keeps it gripping and unpredictable. Altogether in all, 'Hunting Girl' is a major reason why *Songs from the Wood* feels partially like a musical collection of short fiction.

'Ring Out Solstice Bells' (Anderson)

As reported in Paul Rees' essay 'Let's Party Like It's 1399: The Story Behind Jethro Tull's *Songs from the Wood*', Anderson was 'badgered' by their label, Chrysalis, to 'redecorate' this centrepiece as a Christmas single (despite his objections and its overt ties to paganism). In turn, he 'handed it over to Mike Batt, of The Wombles fame, but his Yule-friendly garnish was to no one's taste', so Chrysalis 'chucked out Anderson's original ... whereupon it entered the UK charts at No.28', if only for the first week of December.

Those discordances aside, it's easy to hear why the song was picked for such an occasion and still serves as a staple of the season in the UK. From its merry gusts of woodwinds, acoustic guitar, piano, organ, hand claps, and drums to its harmonised declarations about winter, mistletoe, and bells 'loudly chiming', it encompasses the cheerfulness of Christmastime rather adeptly. This is perhaps most salient during its quiet chorus, when Anderson invites listeners to 'ring out these bells' with inflamed opulence, as if to simulate a grand yuletide gathering. Roughly two minutes in, an orchestral climb results in a powerfully sombre key change of the carol to suggest a subtext of loneliness amidst the otherwise shared jolliness. The outro of bells, percussion, and flutes really get you in the holiday spirit, too.

'Velvet Green' (Anderson)

Detailing a couple's erotic escapades in the English countryside, 'Velvet Green' instantly evokes a stress-free regal air with its main harpsichord recital (alongside bass, bells, flutes, and acoustic guitar frills). The arrangement deepens a growing sense of dread as those other timbres take over with support from Barlow's sundry arsenal. These temperament shifts foreshadow the upset of Anderson's account, as he goes from detailing a sexual cavorting ('Never a care / With your legs in the air') with relaxed thespian gravity to an unkinder and barer decree about his female lover 'walk[ing] home cold and alone' because 'August's rare delight may be April's fool'. In other words, the speaker wants no part of her possible pregnancy once this summertime romp is done. It's a striking shift of character sonically and narratively, and the abrupt count-off into ritualistic instrumental frolicking (via another sublime mishmash of fancifully verdant trade-offs) during the shuffle is flat-out mesmerising.

'The Whistler' (Anderson)

Few, if any, other Jethro Tull songs balance gloomy and gleeful attitudes as authoritatively as this one. Its extraordinarily ominous verse ornamentation – strummed acoustic guitars beneath a foreboding melody that's accentuated by bizarre textures, marimba, and glockenspiel – perfectly complements Anderson's ghostly ringing proclamations ('All kinds of sadness I've left behind me / Many's the day when I have done wrong'). These passages are niftily juxtaposed by a triumphant chorus whose untroubled foundation (featuring faint bites from Barre) raises morale once again. Thus, 'The Whistler' soars with ingenious disparities that are impossible to shake off.

'Pibroch (Cap in Hand)' (Anderson)

Kicked off by Barre's cacophony of razor-sharp howls (meant to imitate bagpipes, as the title implies), Song from the Wood's penultimate inclusion steadily builds violent momentum on which to lay its penitent ode about a man who 'bundles his regrets into a gesture of sorrow' as he discovers his lover having dinner with another man. The playing around Anderson's solemness is tremendously dynamic, as Barre continues his assaults – in conjunction with hyperactive woodwinds and rhythms – in-between the more subdued and discerning environment of organ and strings that coat the verses. The midway deviations – Palmer's initial classical beautification, an ensuing folkish dab of merriment, and a stately electronic/orchestral finale – are wonderfully inspired, too, adding an abundance of different modes to an already fascinating form.

'Fire at Midnight' (Anderson)

As if in direct response to the prior situation, 'Fire at Midnight' is an adoring and comforting acoustic closer – with piano, flutes, militaristic drumming, and alarming yet oddly fitting synthesizers – that sees Anderson returning home after the day's duties are done, caring for his partner, and writing a love song as he 'all too seldom' does. Once more, he and Barre join forces during the break, eventually bringing in Evan for a three-way skirmish of electric guitar, piano, and mandolin assertions. Also, the twice-occurring angelic chant is a suitable but distressing insertion that gives it – and *Songs for the Wood* – eerie closure.

Bonuses

'The Country Set' 40th Anniversary edition of *Songs from the Wood* is probably the most expansive reissue yet (chronologically). Its first CD consists of

Wilson's usual stereo remix and supplementary selections (like the previously unreleased 'Old Aces Die Hard', 'Working John, Working Joe', and 'Strip Cartoon', plus an early version of 'One Brown Mouse' from *Heavy Horses*). The second and third CDs are filled with over twenty live tracks from the American portion of their 1977 tour (remixed by Jakko Jakszyk and recorded on either November 21st or December 6th). The two DVDs contain that November show at the Capital Centre in Landover, Maryland, as well as 5.1 surround, stereo, flat transfer, and quadrophonic mixes of the first CD's material. As a truly seminal album for the band and subgenre, *Songs from the Wood* deserves nothing less.

Heavy Horses (1978)

Personnel:
Ian Anderson: vocals, acoustic guitar, electric guitar, flute, mandolin
Martin Barre: electric guitar, additional material
Barriemore Barlow: drums, percussion
John Glascock: bass guitar, backing vocals
John Evan: piano, organ
Dee Palmer; portative pipe organ, saxophone, other keyboards, orchestral
arrangements, additional material
Darryl Way; violin (2, 8)
Robin Black: engineer
Shona Anderson: back cover, photography
James Cotier: photography
Produced at Maison Rouge Studio, London, May 1977 – January 1978 by Ian
Anderson
UK and US release date: April 1978.
Highest chart places: UK: 20, USA: 19
Running time: 42:25
Current edition: Chrysalis 2018 three-CD/two-DVD 40th Anniversary 'New Shoes'
(Steven Wilson Remixed)

Creatively and critically, *Songs from the Wood* was a reawakening for Jethro
Tull, whose glorious, almost preternatural level of captivating hooks and
delectable sounds helped spearhead a merger of techniques that remains
persuasive. It's no mystery, then, why they chose to tread much of the same
trail on its successor, *Heavy Horses*. The middle child of their official 'folk
rock trilogy', it generally takes a grittier and more efficient route to covering
the same sonic path; as such, it consciously favours bristlier realities over
entrancingly diverse illusions to bid a slightly less special – though very
valuable – continuation with reliably immaculate cohesion.

Diverging from the historical quaintness of its antecedent, Heavy Horses
is rooted in contemporary commentaries about agriculture, an honest day's
work, and the sentimental passage of time. Anderson illuminates by saying
that as a boy, his 'big passion was to get off the leash and explore the local
wooded and leafy suburbs'; thus, those topics weren't new interests as
much as they simply 'fitted what [he] wanted to write about at the time'.
Concurrently, Anderson was settling into domestic life (in a '16th-century
farmhouse in the Buckinghamshire countryside') with his new wife, Shona
(formerly Learoyd), and their son, James Duncan; this newfound comfort and
contemplation inspired his songwriting in ways that conflicted with manager
Terry Ellis, who confesses, 'He and I had some words over some of, well,
what I called the "country" material ... I said to him, "I don't think a kid in
the projects in Detroit can relate to hunting foxes, Ian"'. As always, though,
it's precisely that characteristic authenticity that makes the work so enticing.

Above: Ian Anderson at Catacombs in Houston, TX on 16 Aug 1969 with unknown companion.(*Bruce Kessler*)

Above: Doane Perry, Paul Hamer of Hamer Guitars, and Martin Lancelot Barre outside the Chicago Theatre, Chicago, Illinois on Sunday, 26 June 2011. It was the last official U.S. concert of Jethro Tull before they split. (*Michael Gillett*)

LEFT: Anderson, Abrahams, Cornick and Bunker looking older and dirtier than usual on the front cover of their debut, 1968's *This Was*. *(Rhino Records)*

RIGHT: James Grashow's woodcut front cover for 1969's *Stand Up*, which originally opened like a children's pop-up book. *(Rhino Records)*

LEFT: Jethro Tull window gazing at their own performance on Ruan O'Lochlainn's cover for 1970's *Benefit*. *(Rhino Records)*

RIGHT: Burton Silverman's watercolour (from Jennie Anderson's photograph) of a homeless man on the Thames Embankment for 1971's *Aqualung* is among the most iconic images in all of classic rock. *(Rhino Records)*

LEFT: The full cover of Jethro Tull's 5th studio album, 1972's *Thick as a Brick*, whose satirical design was created by Roy Eldridge. Also included is a full 12-page broadsheet newspaper full of conceptual parodies related to the album's subject matter (co-written by Anderson, Evan, and Hammond-Hammond). *(Chrysalis Records; photo by Stephen Lambe)*

A de GROOT TO GET SPLICED

This week Angela, daughter of Mr. and Mrs. Ferdie D. U. de Groot, announced her engagement to Derek Pith of St. Cleve.

Angela, an effervescent, pretty 17-year-old, is frequently to be seen dancing the latest steps at our local dance hall on a Saturday night. It was at one of these dances that she met Derek. They became friendly while teaching him the latest dance craze from the U.S.A. 'The Crutch'. Naturally, Derek presented himself to be a very slow learner!

Last year Angela left school, full of hopes of becoming an actress. But now says Angela, she is going to concentrate all her time on Derek and the children. Fine sentiments from one so young.

Meanwhile Angela has been working at her father's boutique 'The Brass Knob' which she enjoys doing very much.

Derek, who is a computer programmer, spends all his spare time building sand-castles by the sea. A little unusual, but that is exactly what attracted our little Angela to him. "He's so different", she says dreamily. Every Sunday morning they do to the beach, in all kinds of weather, equipped with bucket and spade. There Derek erects his

Angela de Groot : The Brass Knob keeps her occupied for now but soon she's going to concentrate all her time on Derek and the children.

WOMENS LEAGUE OF PETS

Women's Drama Group Needs New Members

The St. Cleve Amateur Dramatic Society for Women urgently needs new members for their next production 'Mutiny on the Bounty'. Miss Butcher explained that they are hoping to put on this adventurous production before next Easter only

Above: A bit of local romantic gossip within the pages of *Thick as a Brick*'s faux periodical, *The St. Cleve Chronicle & Linwall Advertiser. (Chrysalis Records; photo by Stephen Lambe)*

NON-RABBIT MISSING

Non-Rabbit

One of an experimental batch of non-rabbits is believed to have escaped from a van on the Linwell Road on Monday.

A team of volunteers hunted for it in vain for several hours, and experts think that it may be hiding. The public are requested to be on the look-out for the non-rabbit in the St. Cleve—Linwell Heath area and should notify the police immediately if spotted. Rabbit man Dr. Farley Ruskin commented that it is extremely difficult to tell a non-rabbit from a real one, but the non-rabbit gives off when excited, a glandular secretion with a musky odour which can be harmful to male donkeys and women with sensitive skin. The non-rabbit is thought to be the source of a possible cure for cancer in chimpanzees and rodents it was revealed last month.

Left: A humorous scientific mishap reported in *The St. Cleve Chronicle & Linwall Advertiser. (Chrysalis Records; photo by Stephen Lambe)*

upper
ways.
ower
o come
e l
enty years
vater's
ort and
make

PROF. PANGLOS AND RABBIT

group played all the instruments themselves. In addition to his usual flute, acoustic guitar and singing roles, Ian Anderson extended his virtuosity to violin, sax and trumpet, while Martin Barre played a few lines on that delightful mediaeval instrument, the lute, as well as his electric guitar. John Evan played organ, piano and harpsichord, Jeffrey Hammond-Hammond played bass guitar and spoke some words, and new drummer Barriemore Barlow added the

timpani and percussion parts. One doubts at times the validity of what appears to be an expanding theme throughout the two continuous sides of this record but the result is at worst entertaining and at least aesthetically palatable. Poor, or perhaps naive taste is responsible for some of the ugly changes of time signature and banal instrumental passages linking the main sections but ability in this direction should come with maturity. Taken on the whole however this is a fine disc and a good example of the current pop

★ HOROSCOPE ★

Capricorn Dec 22–Jan 19
This week you may feel the benefit of Venus in your sign; business prospects receive an unexpected bonus. However, you need to get out and about more. Tackle everything with a sparkle. A time when Cupid takes a temporary backseat in your affairs.

Aquarius Jan 20–Feb 18
The pace is slowing up next week and you can how afford to take things at a more leisurely pace. Very

Cancer June 21–July 20
The week ahead continues to be successful for business men. Those in business may even receive several surprising benefits. A good time for outdoor exercise and travel, but forget your love affair for the week. A quiet phase.

Leo July 21–Aug 22
Be careful not to overtax your energy in the week ahead. Romance due to enter a more harmonious and yet vigorous stage—maybe coming into contact with strangers

---

Above: Horoscopes and a comic about anthropomorphic existentialism grace the pages of *The St. Cleve Chronicle & Linwall Advertiser. (Chrysalis Records; photo by Stephen Lambe)*

Below: No paper is complete without a sports section, and *The St. Cleve Chronicle & Linwall Advertiser* is no exception. *(Chrysalis Records; photo by Stephen Lambe)*

St. Cleve Chronicle **11**

FENNEL
Will St.Cleve Fennel again?
FOUR FIELDS FARM 14 OLD CLEVIANS 4

Four Fields Farm gave a much improved performance in their fourth victory over the Old Clevians on Sunday afternoon.

Although four points down at the end of the first quarter, Four Fields Farm fought back magnificently to win 14-4. A crowd of 400 saw them take a grip on the game that never slackened. If it hadn't been for the brave display by John Tetrad, the old Clevians might have finished with a scoreline that read 44-4.

Brian Payne put the Old Clevians ahead four minutes before the end of the first quarter. With a pass from Keith Watson he cleverly beat two men in a very short space; poynted and had the Chervil down before Four Fields knew what had hit them.

A brilliant Fennel by Quad on the restart was just what Four Fields wanted. Quad followed up with two more and nearly had his quarter, but was brilliantly blagged by Tetrad of the old Clevians. From then on little was seen of the old Clevians forwards.

Sent Off
As the game warmed up Fortny and Quad were booked for fouls on Sanderson and Payne. With tempers rising Four Fields looked as if they may lose their grip on the game and it was at this point that Quad was sent off after he produced a spanner with which he threatened the old Clevians Captain, the Reverend John Smythe-Liphook. Quad had to be "assisted" from the field (see photo).

Despite the removal of this valuable player and several disallowed fennels, Four Fields piled on the pressure in all of the other quarters finishing with a spectacular fennel by Fortny four seconds from the final whistle.

The discovery of the mediaeval game of Fennel and its fast growing popularity in and around St. Cleve area is due solely to Mr. John Tetrad, the St. Cleve Librarian and close friend of Lady Parrit of Parrit House. According to Mr. Tetrad the discovery of the game was a complete accident whilst he was browsing through ancient manuscripts concerning the vaulting at the Lady Chapel of Ely Cathedral. Said Mr. Tetrad, "I was glancing at a chapter concerning the Ogee-curved Quatrefoils of the Spandrels at Ely when upon turning a page in the manuscript I found inserted what at first sight looked to be several pages of childrens' scribblings. Upon closer inspection, these pages revealed themselves to be of indeed that nature".

"Encouraged by the knowledge that what I had discovered what was a serious game of skill, I was determined to unfold its mysteries, and bring Fennel back to the public's attention. Now, even at that stage I had no idea of the consequences of this thrilling discovery. Local reaction has been remarkable.

During the last four months, interest has spread not onlyin the St. Cleve area, but as far afield as Linwall Heath."

Mr. Tetrad continued the interview with a fascinating explanation of the rules of play. I have therefore for the many readers who are yet to participate in the game, given a brief résumé of these rules.

Max Quad, being restrained by an umpire after attacking the Rev. John Smythe-Liphook (centre.)

BRIEF RESUME OF THE RULES:—

Players can move the fennels only with the palm of the hand, the thumb being held free. The fennel must not rise above knee height. If there are four fennels in play at any one time these are to be moved to the opposition's end of the field and positioned on one of the four poyntes that are spaced around the field with a diameter of four yards). This procedure is called poynting.

Inside the circum is the chervil which consists of four round stumps of wood each being four feet in height and ranged four inches apart in a straight line. The distance from chervil to chervil will be forty yards.

Upon poynting one of the four fennels the player races inside the circum, spins around on the ball of his foot, and with the other foot breaks the chervil, i.e. disturbs all the four stumps. If however before the player can break the chervil an opponent can disturb the fennel from the poynte, there will be no score and the game shall continue. It must be remembered that meanwhile all the other fennels remain in play even when a fennel is scored. Upon fennelling the fennel is brought back to one of the four centre poynts and play is begun by the side which lost the fennel.

Play is adjudicated by four umpires.

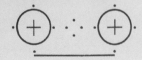

LEFT: Brian Ward's haunting shot of a deceased ballerina (Jane Eve) welcomes you to Jethro Tull's most complex and polarising LP, 1973's *A Passion Play. (Chrysalis Records)*

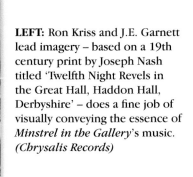

RIGHT: 1974's *War Child* cover exposes a negative image of Anderson in his 'minstrel' outfit superimposed over the skyline of Melbourne, Australia. Many people see it as capturing his 'identification with the typical sarcastic, social commenting fools of Shakespeare's plays'. *(Chrysalis Records)*

LEFT: Ron Kriss and J.E. Garnett lead imagery – based on a 19th century print by Joseph Nash titled 'Twelfth Night Revels in the Great Hall, Haddon Hall, Derbyshire' – does a fine job of visually conveying the essence of *Minstrel in the Gallery*'s music. *(Chrysalis Records)*

RIGHT: Michael Farrell and David Gibbons' illustrated cover for *Too Old to Rock 'n' Roll: Too Young to Die!* It nails the madcap vibe of the album's narrative. *(Chrysalis Records)*

LEFT: 1977's *Songs from the Wood* is delightfully rustic, and so is this main visual from Keith Howard and Jay L. Lee. *(Chrysalis Records)*

RIGHT: James Cotier early morning photo of Anderson leading his *Heavy Horses*. *(Chrysalis Records)*

A scholarly yet rebellious Martin Barre in the 1978 promo video for the 'Heavy Horses' track. *(Chrysalis Records)*.

Ian Anderson looking sinister from the 1977 promo video for 'The Whistler'. *(Chrysalis Records)*

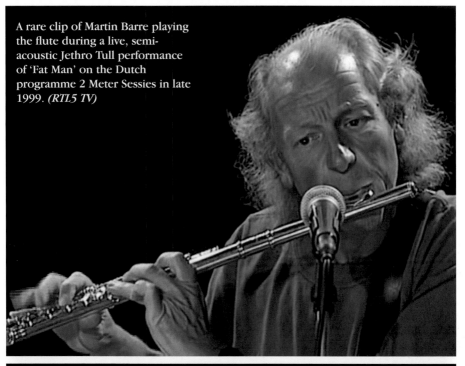

A rare clip of Martin Barre playing the flute during a live, semi-acoustic Jethro Tull performance of 'Fat Man' on the Dutch programme 2 Meter Sessies in late 1999. *(RTL5 TV)*

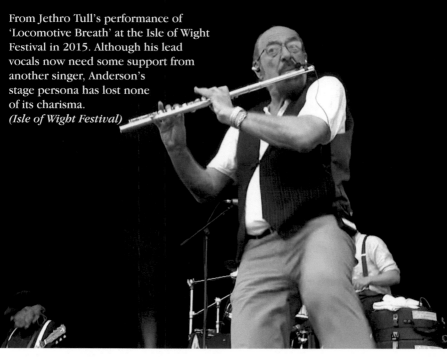

From Jethro Tull's performance of 'Locomotive Breath' at the Isle of Wight Festival in 2015. Although his lead vocals now need some support from another singer, Anderson's stage persona has lost none of its charisma.
(Isle of Wight Festival)

LEFT: David Jackson seems to be depicting Ian Anderson as he watches literal and figurative tempests envelop him on 1979's *Stormwatch*. *(Parlophone)*

RIGHT: *A.* This colourful cover by John Shaw and Martyn Goddard sees the fledgeling line-up charting new territory into a new decade. *(Parlophone)*

LEFT: 1982's *The Broadsword and the Beast* may not be entirely captivating, but its artwork (by Jim Gibson and Iain McCaig) certainly is. *(Parlophone)*

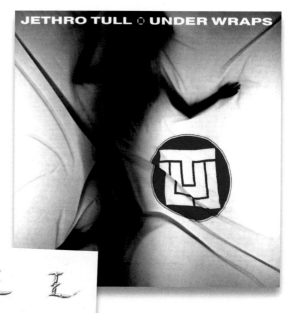

RIGHT: Unlike much of its contents, the figure on Jethro Tull's 1984 collection is wisely kept *Under Wraps*. *(Parlophone)*

LEFT: Martyn Goddard returned (alongside Andrew Jamieson and John Pasche) for this dignified depiction of 1987's *Crest of a Knave*. *(Parlophone)*

RIGHT: 1989's *Rock Island* cover is less timeless, inspired, and exciting than the music it represents. *(Parlophone)*

Poster for Jethro Tull at the Houston Music Hall on 14 May 1970. It's surprisingly colourful and bombastic. *(Bruce Kessler)*

Poster for Jethro Tull at the Catacombs in Houston, TX on 16 Aug 1969. It is a bit reminiscent of the *Stand Up* cover. *(Bruce Kessler)*

A surprisingly accurate Ian Anderson sculpture (polyester but with a layer of very thin gold pieces) by Belgium artist Antoine Bral. *(Guido Verbiest)*.

John Goldacker drew this 1930s Disney-esque tour poster for an October 1996 show in Orlando, FL that was then signed by Ian Anderson. *(John Goldacker)*

LEFT: Even Ian Anderson dislikes the primary image for the band's 1990s album, *Catfish Rising*, due to it having 'too much black! Too much Spinal! No space to sign autographs with a black Sharpie'. *(Parlophone)*

RIGHT: 1995's *Roots to Branches* receives aptly reinvigorated artwork to complement its surprisingly revitalised and varied compositions. *(Parlophone)*

LEFT: Jethro Tull's last proper studio album, 1999's *J-Tull Dot Com*, is far more coherent and intriguing than its main visual (by Martyn Goddard and Bogdan Zarkowski) would have you believe. *(Parlophone)*

RIGHT: Igor Vereshagin's photography perfectly captures the heartwarming nature of 2003's *The Jethro Tull Christmas Album*. *(EMI)*

LEFT: An immensely classy visual companion for 1972's stunning *Living in the Past* compilation. *(Chrysalis Records)*

RIGHT: Ian Anderson *Bursting Out* with his token oversized orange balloon in 1978. *(Chrysalis Records)*

Left: A guest pass to an August 1976 show at Balboa Stadium in San Diego, CA (during the *Too Old to Rock 'n' Roll: Too Young to Die!* Tour) *(Bruce Kessler)*

Right: An *A Passion Play* tour pass for the 15 Jul 1973 show at the Sam Houston Coliseum in Houston, TX *(Bruce Kessler)*

Left: A guest pass for Jethro Tull's show at Madison Square Garden in New York, NY on 10 March 1975, between the releases of *War Child* and *Minstrel in the Gallery (Bruce Kessler)*

Stylistically, *Heavy Horses* sees the sextet purposefully avoiding the rising trends of new musical styles. As Anderson told Rob Hughes in 'Jethro Tull: Keeping the Folk Fires Burning', 'We were keenly aware of not wanting to appear as if we were trying to slip into the post-punk coattails that were worn by The Stranglers or The Police'. In a chat with Philip Wilding, he lingers, 'I don't really recall being moved as a music maker by any of those changes in music that were going on. I knew what it was about and I rather liked some of it, but it was entirely separate to what I was writing. I didn't want to try to catch up or be influenced by it'. Instead, he often chose to write during 'snatched moments' on train rides between the studio and home and stay loyal to his instincts and the heart of Jethro Tull's identity.

While certainly not one of the band's most extravagant or evocative designs, the visuals for *Heavy Horses* nonetheless tangled some manes (figuratively speaking). The front cover was shot in the morning – as 'the threads of sunshine are turning into beams of light' prior to the excessive midday heat – with a telephoto lens, leaving Anderson to 'walk an awful long way' with the titular animals and later conclude, 'It could have been [done] so much easier'. As for the back image – a seemingly candid take of all six members in a well-furnished room, wearing tuxes and drinking wine – it's been speculated as a purposefully conservative inside joke 'at themselves for being comfortable middle-class rockers'. Much like the music it encased, the look of *Heavy Horses* was decidedly unhip yet true to form.

Despite not charting as highly in the US or UK as its forebear, *Heavy Horses* still received a fair number of accolades from the press upon release, although *Melody Maker*'s Harry Doherty remarked: 'I'm forced to compare Tull to an ageing dog: lots of bark but no bite'. *Record Mirror*'s Sheila Prophet somewhat justifiably felt that it was 'very different from the crazed "progressive" outfit [she] used to know and love'. Today, it's held dear by many devotees, not to mention Barre himself, who calls it (in conjunction with *Songs from the Wood*) 'two of the best albums from [his] time in Jethro Tull'. As Anderson surmises, it's 'not quite part two' of *Songs from the Wood*, and its darker dichotomy allows it to simultaneously come across like a kindred spirit to their 1977 classic and a precursor to the storm that would end the era (in more ways than one).

'... And the Mouse Police Never Sleeps' (Anderson)
The moniker makes more sense when you ponder its inspiration – Anderson's cat. It's affectionately tongue-in-cheek the whole way through, with a sustained *Thick as a Brick*-esque breeziness (hypnotic dual acoustic guitar strums, controlled rhythms, and sprinkled woodwinds) racing his tickled observations about his 'bed foot-warmer of purest feline ancestry ... with thoughts of mouse-and-apple pie'. Although dreamily meek, Evan's electronic pronouncement ninety seconds in summons peers like Keith Emerson and Rick Wakeman in its futuristic counterpoints. Also, the closing chants are intimidatingly malicious

given the cheery countrified momentum of the preceding quest (perhaps to suggest the instinctual killer inside of his otherwise fluffy and friendly companion).

'Acres Wild' (Anderson)

Rightly described by Hughes as 'a flaming campfire stand-off', it's is a ritualistic, sexualized, and orthodoxly structured plea 'for better days ahead'. Barlow's light dashes mix well with Anderson's mandolin eagerness and Darryl Way's theatrical screeches on violin. Surprisingly, there's a mild funk/disco thrust to it (especially with Glascock's animated patterns) put side by side with surprising solidity by a sort of farmland hoedown vigour. Add to that a palpable raspiness that Anderson really hadn't showcased since Aqualung – a repeated and defining component of *Heavy Horses*, actually – and you have one of the sequence's most adventurous personalities (even if the principal writing isn't anything to write home about).

'No Lullaby' (Anderson)

The second dedication on the LP (and the lengthiest entry by several minutes), 'No Lullaby' – as you'd guess – was written for James Duncan and uses Barre's token punchiness as a jumping off point. His intricate and irregular interactions with Barlow persist as exciting, of course, and the moody and slow waltz that follows – set off by quick drum fills – affords an arresting change of pace. Anderson's wraithlike coarseness fits perfectly on top of the consequent rapid and erratic ferocity, too, with worrying edicts like 'And let no sleep bring false relief from the tension of the fray / Come wake the dead with the scream of life, do battle with ghosts at play' guiding Barre and Glascock as they quickly hike in unison. Naturally, there's some imposing multitracked guitar soloing within the shuffle, and its perpetual instabilities in disposition keep it exciting as it delivers an atypical (but perfectly fitting for Anderson) method for reassuring an infant.

'Moths' (Anderson)

'Moths' was the only single from *Heavy Horses*, and it's clear why it was chosen. Its acoustic happiness (together with gentle percussion, keyboards, strings, and flutes) evokes the sanguinity of summer rather nicely; it also offsets Anderson's gravely stanzas – no doubt due to him having a cold during some of the recording sessions – with champion poise. The arrangement livens up and becomes even more symphonically utopic prior to a key change before concluding, which, in conjunction with its expectant lyricsm ('And the long night awakened /And we soared on powdered wings / Circling our tomorrows / In the wary month of spring') spawns one of the band's most beautiful pieces in years.

'Journeyman' (Anderson)

Glascock leads this reflection on 'the conformist drudgery of the daily commute' with a forceful loop as bass drum stomps keep the pace, and electric guitar, keyboard, and woodwind outline mesh-like cogs in a wheel. Above them, Anderson tells of 'spine-tingling railway sleepers' who '[slide] through Victorian tunnels' (and other rhyming details that, in emblematic shrewdness, accurately expose the sights, sounds, and feelings of the experience he's conveying). To be frank, this groundwork does get a tad monotonous, yet the instrumental inflections Barre, Palmer,and Anderson augment after each verse keep it sufficiently absorbing. Glascock and Barlow's frenzied aside halfway through is a nice touch, as is the serene respite – with sound effects – that quickly follows. Both repeat before 'Journeyman' ends, too, ensuring that there's always something urbane to latch onto.

'Rover' (Anderson)

Having already penned pieces for his cat and son, Anderson pays tribute to his dog with this sixth selection. Its starting combination of colourfully knotted percussion, organ, and acoustic guitars is undoubtedly one of the record's untouchable flashes – and clearest connections to the bouncy eccentricities of *Songs from the Wood* – and the resultant arpeggiated motif (on which Anderson narrates through the eyes of the canine) is prettily poignant, too. The ways in which the troupe effervescently adorn and modulate around it (including bringing back the maiden assembly) is imaginative and breathtaking as well, guaranteeing that it gets stuck in your head long after it's over.

'One Brown Mouse' (Anderson)

An obvious companion to '... And the Mouse Police Never Sleeps', it's a chipper acoustic contribution that centres on Anderson's echoed and high-spirited vocals ('Smile your little smile / Take some tea with me awhile'). Meanwhile, an influx of peaceful drums, piano, strings, and bass advance little by little toward a heartier bridge ('Do you wonder if I really care for you?') and wordless curve of imperial synths, flutes, syncopation, and other dazzling knick-knacks. It's a wistful tangent that once again validates Jethro Tull's expertise at taking listeners on ephemeral yet exquisite voyages in-between the homeland bookends of the song itself.

'Heavy Horses' (Anderson)

It's not as ambitious and irresistible as some previous title tracks (not that it needs to be), but 'Heavy Horses' is thrilling all the same. Led by Barre, Anderson, and Glascock's alluringly aligned flow around the chorus, it's an enthusiastic dirge about how 'times will change. They'll be gone and won't be coming back', so we must 'treasure them while they're still here'. The elaborate beginning acts almost like an overture before succulent piano and strings provide the only accompaniment for dramatically harmonised poeticisms such as 'The Suffolk, the Clydesdale, the Percheron vie / With the Shire on his feathers floating / Hauling soft timber into the dusk / To bed on a warm straw coating'. It's a beguilingly mournful counterbalance to the rousing chorus, and the switch of piano for an acoustic guitar for the ensuing segment is subtle yet significant. Afterwards, Palmer and Way clutch the spotlight with a hurried classical curve (reinforced mostly by tight percussive notes) that soon rests underneath the song proper. When they finish, Barre instructs with his customary gusto as Barlow resourcefully stampedes to loftier reprisals of erstwhile brews (including a faux conclusion about six minutes in). All things considered, it's the showiest serving on *Heavy Horses* by a mile and a meaningful epic in its own right.

'Weathercock' (Anderson)
There's a surreal and appeasing innocence to the courtship of acoustic guitar fingerpicking and keyboard meditation here, just as Anderson's gruff biddings – 'Give us direction / The best of goodwill / Put us in touch with fair winds' – emanate folkish charm and yearning. Then, the arrival of thunderous beats, frisky portative pipe organ twirls, and elastic bass mandates punctuate with pagan liveliness until it converts into a hard rock base that warrants Anderson and Glascock's provokingly heartfelt interlude. At the apex (following another chorus), this part returns with extra oomph from Barre's mounting governance, fading out *Heavy Horses* with opaque and motivational catharsis. It's easily among their most vital album climaxes.

Bonuses
Another five-disc 'bookset' substantiates the 'New Shoes' edition of Heavy Horses with an equivalent range of extras as kept in the 'Country Set' of Songs from the Wood. There's the requisite stereo, 5.1 surround, flat transfer, and quadraphonic mixes of the album and associated recordings – covering 'Quatrain', 'Everything in our Lives', and two versions of 'Living in These Hard Times', among other riches – in addition to the complete 'Live in Concert: Berne, Switzerland, May 1978' audio (mixed by Jakko Jakszyk in stereo, 5.1 DTS, and surround sound) and videos for 'Heavy Horses', 'Moths', and two advertisements for 1978's *Bursting Out*. It's a properly bulky assortment, to say the least.

Stormwatch (1979)

Personnel:
Ian Anderson: vocals, acoustic guitar, flute, bass guitar (1, 3, 4, 5, 6, 7, 8)
Martin Barre: electric guitar, mandolin, classical guitar
Barriemore Barlow: drums, percussion
John Glascock: bass guitar (2, 9, 10)
John Evan: piano, organ
Dee Palmer: portative pipe organ, orchestral arrangements, synthesizers, saxophone
Francis Wilson: spoken voice (1, 8)
Robin Black: engineer
Leigh Mantle: engineer
David Jackson: artwork
Peter Wragg : art direction
Produced at Maison Rouge Studio, London, Spring 1979 – Summer 1979 by Ian Anderson and Robin Black
UK and US release date: Spring 1979.
Highest chart places: UK: 27, USA: 22
Running time: 45:42
Current edition: Parlophone 2004 remastered CD

The final chapter in the 'folk rock trilogy' – and the final Jethro Tull studio conception of the decade – *Stormwatch* was made during arguably the squalliest phase in their history, and the resulting exoduses of Barlow, Evan, Glascock, and Palmer means that it marked the last effort by the 'classic' late 1970s line-up. There's a melancholic soul to much of the album that corresponds to its internal and external overcasts; yet, for something that spawned out of such a tumultuous time, it houses an explicitly smooth tide (that its centrepiece and concluding instrumentals act as intrinsic thematic glue surely subsidises that distinction). Hence, it's a crucial release from a historical perspective alone, and while it doesn't rival *Songs from the Wood* or even *Heavy Horses* on a song-by-song chart, it's emotional and satisfactorily inventive fluidity – with some nautical drops to boot – makes it a worthy cap off to the period.

Glascock's pervasive health problems were the chief behind-the-scenes issues surrounding *Stormwatch*, with Barre later disclosing, 'Making [it] was a horrible period of time because of John being ill. It all started going really badly in the studio and it wasn't his fault. Every band member was to blame to some extent. The album really shouldn't have happened. You can hear the struggle, musically, to get it made'. Diagnosed with a cardiac infection from a congenital heart defect within only the preceding year or so (making him unable to finish the American side of the *Heavy Horses* tour), Glascock continued living wildly while his condition worsened. Following a few warnings, Anderson fired him and took over most of the bass playing duties.

As he explains,

> *There was a lot of stress within the band ... We sent [John] home and told him he had to get out of this spiral he was in because it wasn't just his illness, it was his lifestyle. He'd be on stage and his face would be white like wax, with a film of sweat. Unfortunately, he had a bunch of folks around him who were not strong characters themselves. I really feel they made it too easy for him to carry on doing drink, drugs, late nights and parties.*

On November 17, 1979, Glascock passed away, and when Anderson found out, he understandably felt mixed emotions about the separation. Looking back, he postulates, 'Did we do everything we could to help? That's a question we'll ask ourselves forever'. (The situation also played a part in the partings of the other three members, but since that happened after *Stormwatch* was released, it'll be discussed later.)

Anderson adds that even if Glascock's illness and illicit activities weren't factors, Stormwatch 'would have come out' the same way because of 'the mood of the songs'. In keeping with the subject matter of the preceding two entries in the 'folk rock' trio, the LP's 'foreboding tone' derives from its focus on monetary and environmental woes, as well as its historical and legendary allusions. As Rabey designates, it's 'written around a concept ... [that] considers the anxious challenges of the omnipresent energy shortage, paying special attention to our rapidly dwindling oil supplies and the risk of annihilation from nuclear disaster'. Anderson, in a conversation with Wilding, annotates, '[It] was very much about issues of conservation, climate change. You must also remember that the album came at a time when the scientific thinking of the day was that we were verging towards the likelihood of a mini ice age, so that was the driving force behind some of the songs on the album. Once the ice core samples started coming out in the '80s, the scientific community had to rethink this'. Although not a totally bleak downer, Stormwatch ends the set on a considerably darker tone than the 'upbeat' and 'whimsical' tenor that began it.

With a front cover that (no doubt unintentionally) could be seen as depicting its mastermind watching the literal and figurative tempests that enveloped him, Stormwatch faced many pressing issues in and outside of itself. Again, though, those circumstances earn the end result even more veneration for being such a gratifying culmination of multiple realisations. Justly dubbed 'a cohesive curtain call for the band's trademark prog-folk style' and 'the last souvenir of the band's most fruitful period' by Ryan Reed (in his write-up 'How Jethro Tull Ended the '70s with the underrated *Stormwatch*'), it is absolutely a worthwhile – if weaker – companion to *Songs from the Wood* and *Heavy Horses*. Even more, it's a vastly agreeable and expressive swansong before a new decade and ensemble would bring about A predominantly altered Jethro Tull.

'North Sea Oil' (Anderson)

With lyrics like 'Riggers rig and diggers dig their shallow grave / But we'll be saved and what we crave / In North Sea Oil', it's not hard to decipher Anderson's pointed ecological surveillances here. Auspiciously, his sedative singing brands them as enticing and welcoming rather than preachy or maudlin. Equally, its unified electric guitar and flute riff recurs like the coastal core of the blueprint, intermittently chiming in with hearty conquests beside the sprightly rhythmic duo of Barlow and Anderson. Barre and Anderson's characteristic instrumental clashes are still quite electrifying, too, in spite of them being awaited prerequisites at this point. All in all, it's a vivacious bolt of green outspokenness that seduces straightaway.

'Orion' (Anderson)

'Orion' is a two-headed nod to the hunter Nimród – as he's known in the modern Hungarian myth – whose lore inspired the famous constellation. The song stimulatingly oscillates between a combative meter (in which Anderson commands, 'Orion, won't you give me your star sign?' over belligerent percussion and stubborn bass and guitar notes) and crestfallen acoustic passages (whose out-of-synch repeats rest on top of luscious strings from Palmer and chords from Evan). Each round offers minor modifications, too, breeding a startling dyad out of what could've easily been a tedious exercise.

'Home' (Anderson)

'Home' has sometimes been called Jethro Tull's exemplary power ballad, and while that's usually meant in a pejorative sense, it's not entirely unfitting, either. For instance, its verses – while charmingly genuine from a melodic standpoint – could be seen as syrupy given the way lines such as 'As the dawn sun breaks over sleepy gardens / I'll be here to do all things to comfort you' meld into Queen-esque double-tracked electric guitar wails, self-pitying rhythms, and idealistic orchestration. That said, it's just as easy to be bewitched by the gorgeous and relatable candour with which each member encourages the others in a collective outpouring of romance and redemption. I'll always sit on the latter side.

'Dark Ages' (Anderson)

The suite of *Stormwatch*, its nine-minute marathon is packed with the kind of feverish aberrations you'd imagine in something based on such an austere time in Western European history. It commences with worrying scope, too, as defeated, phantom, and scant instrumentation attacks Anderson's avowals. It wisely builds toward his bellowing chorus, however, with yelping guitars and strings jolting around every turn. Before long, Barre and Barlow's locomotive segue boosts the sextet into a faster phase in which tight harmonies rule, 'Come and see bureaucracy / Make its final heave / And let the new disorder through / While senses take their leave'. The moderately peculiar jam that comes next is tempting as well – with enough back-and-forth showmanship between woodwinds, guitar, and bass to be enthrallingly tense – and the subsequent stages of interlocking voices, strings, piano, and electronic tones are haunting breathers before the abrasive last measures. Overall, it's the slight adjustments to each cycle which impress most.

'Warm Sporran' (Anderson)
'Warm Sporran' (named after the pouch on a male Scottish Highland dress) is fittingly fashionable as a wordless piece from 1979 since it melds traditional Middle Eastern and Celtic traces with disco/new wave rhythms. The mountaineer chants bring even more Gaelic authenticity to its influx of flutes, mandolin, classical guitar, bagpipes, and trooping percussion. In that way, it's synchronously at home and alien on a Jethro Tull release, and while it could be more striving to sustain interest, its seaside shanty elicitations definitely tie into *Stormwatch*'s demonstration of how willing Anderson and company were to introduce something fairly fresh into their formula.

'Something's on the Move' (Anderson)
In stark contrast to the prior composition, this one is an unabashedly conventional rocker draped in bristly guitar riffs and urgent judgments ('The lady of the ice sounds / A deathly distant rumble / To Titanic-breaking children lost / In melting crystal tears'). Interestingly, that part actually channels the chorus of 'Bungle in the Jungle'. Aside from some dim keyboard and woodwind embellishments, plus durable playing from Barlow and Anderson (on bass), there's not much more to say about its enjoyable but average edifice.

'Old Ghosts' (Anderson)
The ambience of apparitions blows across the initial acoustic strums, piano taps, bass lines, and rebounded flute spirals at the start. Palmer then guides the disturbing plot ('And young children falter in their games / At the altar of life's hide-and-seek / Between tall pillars, where Sunday-night killers / In grey raincoats peek') with understated philharmonic grace. Likewise, Barre's power-driven stabs centre Anderson's bubblier digressions as the rest of the group preserves course. Despite its mainstream foundation, 'Old Ghosts' remains engaging thanks to its otherworldly textural resonances (especially during the dense outro) and healing major sentiment ('I'll be coming again like an old dog in pain / Blown through the eye of the hurricane / Down to the stones where old ghosts play'). Naturally, the link between its subject and Glascock's situation at the time – whether intentional or not – adds a moving layer.

'Dun Ringill' (Anderson)
In a conversation with Polly Glass for *PROG*, Opeth mastermind Mikael Åkerfeldt cited *Stormwatch*, and 'Dun Ringill' in particular, as an influence

on 'Will O the Wisp' from 2016's *Sorceress*. He wanted to 'write a song with a capo, up high on the fretboard, because it brings a nice "ringy" sound to the guitar', and after listening to Anderson's jingle – titled after an Iron Age hill fort in Scotland – it's easy to tell why Åkerfeldt adores it. A patchwork of predictions from meteorologist Francis Wilson provides the set-up for acoustic arpeggios and chords that happen upon you like a substitute version of *Thick as a Brick*'s most recognisable motif. It's almost as if he's plagiarising himself, yet the spectral nuances and optimistic words ('In the wee hours I'll meet you / Down by Dun Ringill / Oh, and we'll watch the old gods play') assuage that transgression to an extent. Either way, it's a lovely little tune.

'Flying Dutchman' (Anderson)
The last of the fable-inspired inclusions on *Stormwatch*, it alludes to the doomed ghost ship sailing indefinitely with pensive composure at first. A piano recital paints a tastefully nostalgic picture to be doctored with woodwind and electric guitar outbursts. Evan's lamentations linger around Anderson's aptly dejected remembrances – 'Children on the cold sea swell / Not fishers of men / Gone to chase away the last herring / Come empty home again' – with the emotional enormity of a classic Elton John requiem. It's devastating in its emptiness – that is, until the chorus enlivens with victorious instrumentation that partially bleeds into the ensuing verses. Already, it's among the most refined and touching sequences on the record. The juxtaposition between that milieu (which returns with grief-stricken strings near the end, as you might anticipate) and the jubilance of the second half (which finds Glascock holding his own against a maritime march of flute, drums, mandolin, guitar riffs, bagpipes, and more) is as attractive as it is clever. 'Flying Dutchman' may just be the standout selection of them all.

'Elegy' (Palmer)
Written by Palmer for his father – and not for Glascock, as was commonly alleged at the time – 'Elegy' captures the elegant Canterbury dispirit of early Camel or Mike Oldfield, as well as King Crimson's *Islands*. It's a heart-breaking hodgepodge of mirrored phrases in which woodwinds, strings, piano, and classical guitar congregate around a resolute rhythm, evoking the finality of a tragic film's end credits (or, more accurately, the sobering farewell of an album, a decade, a line-up, and an inimitable phase of Jethro Tull). Thus, it's a tenderly bittersweet bid to many losses at once, underpinning the interior and exterior significance of *Stormwatch*.

Bonuses
A Stitch In Time (Anderson)
A quirky rocker with fervent female backing vocals, 'A Stitch in Time', released as a single in 1978, like many Jethro Tull tracks of the time, juxtaposes

moments of stylishly decorated modesty with anxious bursts of instrumental outrage. Evan's piano patterns, while faint, are essential to keeping the rest of the group on task, and while it's not especially invigorating melodically, Anderson's layered voice is sufficiently commanding.

As of this writing, Wilson is working his magic on an expanded treatment for *Stormwatch*, so the most current version is simply a 2004 release with four bonus tracks: 'A Stitch in Time', 'Crossword', 'Kelpie', and 'King Henry's Madrigal'. The second song is a more dynamic and flashy offering. The third (which references a shape-shifting water spirit that occupies Scotland lochs) is properly Celtic and feisty; and the fourth (a reimagining of King Henry VIII's 'Pastime with Good Company') is a pleasingly stately instrumental with many highlights as Anderson, Barre, and Evan ceaselessly complement each other with determined flamboyance. They're all worthy accompaniments to the collection.

A (1980)

Personnel:

Ian Anderson: vocals, acoustic guitar, flute, mandolin
Martin Barre: electric guitar
Dave Pegg: bass guitar, backing vocals
Mark Craney: drums, percussion
Eddie Jobson: keyboards, electric violin, synthesizer, additional material
James Duncan Anderson: vocals (6)
Robin Black: engineer
Leigh Mantle: assistant engineer
John Shaw: photography
Martyn Goddard: photography
Peter Wragg: art direction
Produced at Maison Rouge Mobile and Maison Rouge Studios in Fulham, London,
Summer 1980 by Ian Anderson and Robin Black
UK release date: August 1980. US release date: September 1980.
Highest chart places: UK: 25, USA: 30
Running time: 42:30
Current edition: Parlophone 2004 CD/DVD remastered

As the first studio project of a new decade and an almost completely new line-up, Jethro Tull's 13th album, A, had a lot to prove. After all, the absences of Glascock, Barlow, Evan, and Palmer, coupled with the mushrooming musical tastes and technologies of the 1980s, predestined a marginal, if not hefty, revolution in technique. In addition, such a dramatic swing in players meant possibly losing many fans who held dear the past team and were unlikely to accept a mostly untested cast (had the internet existed back then, hashtags of #notmyjethrotull may have run rampant across it). It's very fortunate, then, that A wound up an appropriate and promising first impression of the newest flight from Anderson's base. Admittedly, A doesn't match any of the 'folk rock trilogy', let alone their peak works of the early 1970s, but it nevertheless vindicated the troupe furthering onward after such drastic departures.

Of course, A was not initially meant to be a new Jethro Tull record at all; rather, the A stood for Anderson's planned debut solo outing (which would finally come three years later, with *Walk into Light*) following the aftermath of the strained *Stormwatch* sessions and tour. Specifically, Barlow left immediately after the tour 'due to depression over the death of John Glascock as well as plans to start his own band', while Evan and Palmer exited to form Tallis after reading a premature – but not incorrect – report of their impending dismissals from *Melody Maker*. In his book *Jethro Tull: A History of the Band, 1968 – 2001*, Scott Allen Nollen quotes Evan as he somewhat bitterly recalls receiving a letter from Anderson that read: 'I'm going to do something on my own, maybe called Jethro Tull, maybe not. But I am using different people and I thought I ought to let you know'. In contrast, Palmer viewed the separation as a 'mixed blessing' that was ultimately a 'necessary' step toward becoming 'a serious composer, arranger and conductor' with his own voice. 'In many ways, elements within the band were growing apart ... It wasn't like it was fragmenting or we were having big fights, it was just a sense of people heading in different directions', Anderson concluded, adding, 'I got to the point where I thought: "Okay, probably best to put this on ice for a time now and do something different"'.

With that chaos somewhat settled, Anderson could concentrate on the first collection he'd tether to his own name. To help, he enlisted the already established violinist/keyboardist Eddie Jobson after seeing him play with U.K. every night during the Stormwatch tour (Jobson's extraordinary work with Curved Air, Roxy Music, and Frank Zappa also helped). Similarly, Mark Craney's stints with Tommy Bolin and Jean Luc-Ponty allowed him to become 'the first American ever to infiltrate the solidly British ranks of Tull'. Jobson is quick to clarify that neither he nor Craney knew that they'd eventually be working on a Jethro Tull album: 'Ian called me in 1980 and asked if I would like to collaborate with him on a solo album. I was just beginning my own solo album, The Green Album, at the time ... I asked [him] if I should bring along Mark Craney – the drummer I was then rehearsing with for my project. Ian agreed and the A album was born'. In hindsight, Craney boasts that it was 'a really creative period' for him and a surprisingly relaxing one (compared to vibe of Los Angeles, where 'the clock is running and everybody is stressing').

Although Jobson and Craney were unquestionably strong choices as session musicians, it's the addition of Fairport Convention bassist Dave Pegg that's the most significant. Having officially replaced Glascock during the Stormwatch tour, he was a clear pick to play on A as well since (as Anderson reflects) his 'musical tradition ... [was] not too dissimilar from our own' and he'd learned a lot of discipline while playing 'huge stadium venues' for the first time. Add in Barre as Anderson's right-hand man and it's not too shocking that, upon hearing of A, Chrysalis successfully persuaded Anderson to rebrand it as a new Jethro Tull LP (a decision he now regrets) due to that inherent marketability (their sales were down at the time, too).

Luckily, making A – whose agenda revolves around 'warning against' the 'anarchy' of 'real-life scenarios, not so much about relationships, but more about things, about realities, about world-scale phenomena' – was a prolific and pleasant process. Anderson reminisces that he wrote many songs 'in the morning, and [they] would be based on whatever was on the news programs the night before'. He expounds: 'And the whole album was done in the ... spirit of ... great rush ... that wonderful feeling with the first cup of coffee, when you actually get a song going and you know you're going to rehearse it that morning, you're going to arrange it in the afternoon, and record it in the evening.'

For sure, A marks a palpable infusion of the digital undercurrents that would become symbolic of the era, yet it's not as much of a contentious and startling deviation as many devotees report. Let's not forget that Stormwatch already bridged a compromise between Jethro Tull's signature progressive rock and folk embellishments and burgeoning bits of new wave-influenced hard rock, so A actually fits well as the next logical step. Even Jobson states that while he understands 'why the "futuristic" approach didn't sit too well with everyone', it was 'meant to be different – and serve as a colourful departure in the long view'. If nothing else, A deserves credit for successfully merging the old and new while maintaining a fair amount of quality and dignity (something that can't be said for several of Jethro Tull's prog rock peers). In other words, Jethro Tull had now entered the 1980s without succumbing too much to its dated proclivities – at least, for now.

'Crossfire' (Anderson)
Jobson's swift keyboard preface, matched with Pegg's rubbery accents and Craney's shrill taps, instantaneously pulls Jethro Tull out of the mythical past and into a modernised setting. Even so, their assets appease and reinvigorate a formula that feels markedly typical thanks to Barre and Anderson's upheld penchants. 'Dealing with law and disorder in ... London, particularly an attack on Britain's Iranian Embassy', the songwriting and structure of 'Crossfire' – like most of the other tracks here – are relatively mechanical and un-nuanced, but the lyrics and instrumentation still intrigue with discerning minutiae. It's definitely more commercial and antiquated (in terms of its slight '80s production) than what came before it, yet it retains enough of the fundamental Jethro Tull DNA to work.

'Fylingdale Flyer' (Anderson)
It's no mystery why this single is also one of the most memorable sections of A considering the seductive gimmick of its stacked vocals. Such immensity is also used to convey the importance of its impetus: a Royal Air Force radar base in England whose BMEWS (Ballistic Missile Early Warning System) alerts the US and UK about impending nuclear doom. Lyrics like 'Through clear skies tracking lightly from far down the line / No fanfare, just a blip on the screen / No quick conclusions, now everything will be fine / Short circuit glitch and not what it seems' bring those fears to life, as do the characteristically off-kilter rock rhythms and riffs that flood the latter half. There's continued playfulness in-between, too, as flute and keyboard reiterate the main theme with saccharine gentleness. It's a terrific attachment from every angle.

'Working John, Working Joe' (Anderson)
'Reflecting on the nature of England's "socialist" welfare state', this other single from A is, well, largely mediocre at best. Granted, Anderson's confessional grit – 'When I was a young man (as all good tales begin) / I was taught to hold out my hand / And for my pay I worked an honest day' – and Barre's fiery ripostes do evoke older gems; but, apart from those flashes of earlier greatness, there's almost nothing to draw you in musically or melodically. In fact, it's among the most all-around rudimentary configurations they'd crafted up to this point,

even if the Barre and Jobson do offer some momentarily dreamy theatricality around the three-minute mark.

'Black Sunday' (Anderson)

The most ultramodern and larger-than-life song on the full-length, 'Black Sunday' begins with sleek ominousness as Jobson fuses multiple synthesised effects and notes into a mass of Draconian engineering that would've fit well on the soundtracks of *1984* and *Blade Runner*. Barre, Pegg, and Craney back him up modestly until Anderson joins in for a thrillingly sinister gambol before it all disappears so that Anderson can hastily recite his vivid account ('Tomorrow is the one day I would change for a Monday / With freezing rains melting and no trains running / And sad eyes passing in windows flimsy'). Jobson's piano playing is a fascinating luxury from start to end, and Barre and Anderson still make quite a pair during their emotive shared solo. Lastly, the reuse of the opening dystopia within the madness, while predictable, is an exceptional slice of classic Jethro Tull ingenuity notwithstanding.

'Protect and Survive' (Anderson)

This side two starter is a spiritual sibling to 'Fylingdale Flyer' in that it's a critique of the Protect and Survive movement enacted by the British government that consisted of pamphlets, radio broadcasts, and public information films about how to make it through a nuclear attack. The idea that a nuclear attack could be survived was predictably contentious, leading Anderson to reprimand the politicians as 'self-appointed guardians of the race / With egg upon their face' as he sings about a postman, milkman, and paper man who 'didn't call' because they died. Honestly, it's one of the most sorrowfully riveting songs Anderson ever shaped, as the catchy verses radiate profound fretfulness and are abetted by a stunning blend of raw complexity, forlorn vocal layers, and shimmering timbres. Each aspect is spellbinding and stirring, making it the true highpoint of *A*.

'Batteries Not Included' (Anderson)

James Duncan makes his recording debut near the end, offering some inquisitive narration to conduct the childlike wonderment effectively – and then panicked disappointment – of finding 'a Japanese toy' on Christmas morning only to then grasp that you can't relish its 'lights that flash' and 'wheels that go round' because there are no batteries. The score supports that takeaway, with a bombastic basis resting beneath Jobson's robotic, video game-esque tapestries to crop a tolerably middling – and slightly irritating – outcome. Anderson's uninspired act doesn't make it less disposable, either.

'Uniform' (Anderson)

Anderson's branded irreverence is once again on display in 'Uniform', another take it or leave it option that sees him deriding the ways in which people lose themselves in their quests to dress up as who they think they should be. Despite some nice woodwind and violin flourishes from him and Jobson, as well as Pegg's distinguishing canter (which conjures early Kate Bush), it's too elementary to be noteworthy.

'4.W.D. (Low Ratio)' (Anderson)
Although adequately agreeable on the surface (with nice piano chords throughout and an exciting instrumental break toward the finale), it comes across as the most effortless – and therefore, worst – entry on *A*. The computerised cheesiness of the call-and-response chorus is the greatest offender, but the wide-ranging affair is unusually negligible, lacking the depth and creativity Jethro Tull were able to muster on many of the contributions that surround this dud. Don't be flabbergasted if Supertramp's vastly superior 'Take the Long Way Home' starts playing in your head as you listen.

'The Pine Marten's Jig' (Anderson)
Thankfully, this penultimate instrumental restores magnitude to the album by presenting a very tricky and folkish romp (as if to say, 'We've not lost the traditional bravura you all love!'). Really, it's a bit incongruous to the set, yet that's precisely what makes it so welcome (and what makes *A* satisfyingly varied). Anderson and Barre, in particular, recall their late '60s / early '70s rural eruptions and exchanges. The newcomers hold their own, too, with Craney and Pegg's go-getting enterprise ensnaring Jobson's violin virtuosity at every turn. As such, it's *A*'s superlative diagram of how efficaciously they work together.

'And Further On' (Anderson)
Whereas much of *A* is direct in its delivery and purpose, closer 'And Further On' is ingeniously enigmatic. It evolves cleverly from an ethereal plane (sparse piano and flute notes amidst shaking cymbals and oppressive synths) to a moving taste of rock opera opulence – and then back again . Anderson's reverberated and loving rhymes ('Before the last faint light has gone / Wish you goodbye till further on / Will you still be there further on?') enhance the spectral veneer. It's an evocative close whose remnants stay after *A* goes silent.

Bonuses
The only supplement to the 2004 remaster is the Slipstream DVD. Recorded in November 1980 at the Los Angeles Sports Arena, it's a mixture of concert footage (featuring but not limited to 'Heavy Horses', 'Locomotive Breath/Black Sunday (reprise)', and 'Songs from the Wood') and music videos directed by David Mallett (including 'Fylingdale Flyer', 'Sweet Dream', and 'Dun Ringill'). Clearly, it's a valuable commemoration of the one-off A quintet.

The Broadsword and the Beast (1982)

Personnel:
Ian Anderson: vocals, acoustic guitar, flute, Fairlight CMI
Martin Barre: electric guitar, acoustic guitar
Dave Pegg: bass guitar, backing vocals, mandolin
Gerry Conway: drums, percussion
Peter-John Vettese: backing vocals, keyboards, piano, synthesiser, additional material
Robin Black: engineer
Leigh Mantle: assistant engineer
Jim Gibson: artwork
Iain McCaig: illustrations, artwork
Produced at Maison Rouge Studios in Fulham, London, Winter 1981 by Paul Samwell-Smith
UK and US release date: April 1982
Highest chart places: UK: 27, USA: 19
Running time: 38:49
Current edition: Parlophone 2005 CD remastered

For the most part, *A* saw Jethro Tull entering the era without succumbing to too much of the inorganic and tacky sheen that plagued much of popular music around that time. Sure, there were traces of that scattered around – and the scripts were often more ordinary and on-the-nose than on older ventures – but there was sufficient idiosyncratic profundity and sing-along magnetism to make it likeable as a package. Sadly, *The Broadsword and the Beast* (their first LP not to be released the year after its predecessor) fares noticeably worse in those areas. By no means terrible – there are still shades of the beloved Jethro Tull persona – its sterile production and paltry songwriting make it a generally subpar attempt.

The Broadsword and the Beast is the only Jethro Tull studio work produced by founding Yardbirds bassist Paul Samwell-Smith (who'd previously produced Cat Stevens, Renaissance, and Carly Simon, among others, and who shouldn't bear all of the blame for the band adapting their sound to the shifts of the period). He came aboard because Anderson 'really [wanted] someone else to come in and mix ... and [take] a lot of pressure off [him]'; providentially, they ended up 'bouncing off each other very well'. To be fair, the album's 'cross between the synthesiser sound of the 1980s and the folk-influenced style ... [of] the previous decade' is pleasurably convivial and lavish in spots.

Seeing as how Jobson and Craney were never official members to begin with (again, they weren't even hired to play on a Jethro Tull record initially), it's no marvel that they aren't here (leaving Pegg as the only A newcomer to stick around). In their absence, session players Peter-John Vettese and Gerry Conway (who also worked with Stevens and is currently in Fairport Convention) took over keyboard and drum duties, respectively. It's worth noting that Conway was replaced by Paul Burgess of 10cc for the subsequent tour but came back a few years later; also, Vettese wasn't there at the start so Anderson 'did the first tracks'.

Regarding the title and cover art (perhaps the two most unforgettable aspects of *The Broadsword and the Beast*), it was 'going to be called Beastie'; however, the group shortly 'deliberated over the preference between Beastie and Broadsword', ultimately agreeing to combine them in the moniker and 'give each side its own title and ... identity' (much like *Aqualung*). As for the imagery (whose emphasis on the former noun leads 'many owners and fans [to] refer to it as the Broadsword album'), it was inspired by C. S. Lewis' *The Voyage of the Dawn Treader*, filled with Easter eggs from McCaig (who was already an immense fan upon commission), and tried 'to capture the concept of the music'. For example, the 'symbols around the edge ... are from the Cirth rune system' and relate to the words of 'Broadsword'.

Just as the release represented an increasingly tangible move away from Jethro Tull's most adored formulas, so too did it end their streak of colossal concerts. As Rabey reports, the tour was preceded by 'rumours floating around' about their obsolescence and resulted in 'the last time [they] averaged 16,000 seaters in North America. From here on in, nothing would bring [them] back into the public eye at the level to which they had been accustomed'. As usual, though, Barre took it all in stride, later commenting that although they'd 'received bad press throughout' it, they kept going because people kept wanting to see them.

Purportedly, there was myriad material for a double sequence, which only makes the quality of the final ten selections more baffling (much of the unused work appeared on later EPs and anniversary assemblages). Anderson may claim that The Broadsword and the Beast contains some of Jethro Tull's top moments; Steven Hackett may favour it; Barre may repute it as 'the first Tull album he truly enjoyed recording'; and the sales may have topped those of Stormwatch and A, but the press has been unanimously cold toward it all along. Unfortunately, time hasn't done it any benefits, either, as it feels too much like a bland relic of its time. Still, it's not wholly insignificant, and it's certainly stronger than what they'd produce two years later, when they became fully draped up in emblematic '80s gaudiness.

'Beastie' (Anderson)

In the press release for *The Broadsword and the Beast*, Anderson remarks that the song is about fear, explaining, 'When I was a boy growing up in Scotland, we called anything that was particularly nasty that we didn't like a Beastie'. His cautionary premonitions of the titular foe as 'your private nightmare pricking' do a fine job of conveying bold trepidation, as do the threatening rhythmic thumps, grating electric guitar cuts, and synth swirls that encircle his barks. At most, it's a decent way to begin and a fun anthem to an unmade horror movie, yet it also reveals the record's partiality for shallow tunes.

'Clasp' (Anderson)
'A song about people who shy away from physical contact', this one finds
the group toying with the idea of giving benevolent handshakes to strangers
('Meeting as the tall ships do, passing in the channel / Afraid to chance a
gentle touch, afraid to make the clasp'). Its bookended angelic and gloomy
atmosphere is set up well so that Conway's looping syncopation can steer
various textures to dissipate around Anderson's pressing decrees; in doing so,
the quintet provides enough quick-witted ornamentation to mostly compensate
for some tawdry production and a lack of rousing songwriting.

'Fallen on Hard Times' (Anderson)
Although its mandolin fingerpicking, slide guitar yowls, and multi-layered choruses
deliver folkish charisma, the disillusioned observations of 'Fallen on Hard Times'
suffers too much from token '80s power ballad compression and triviality. It's
far from insufferable or the worst of its kind – even low-grade Jethro Tull gathers
something to appreciate – but it's overwhelmingly generic nonetheless and overtly
below what they were capable of. (It does, however, beat the reimagining by
Finnish heavy metal quartet Northern Kings on 2007's *Reborn*.).

'Flying Colours' (Anderson)
There's an undeniably bittersweet Christmastime ambience to the opening
piano chords that suits its assessment of quarrelsome lovers who 'revel in
digging up the dirt in front of an audience'. Anderson's lucid miseries ('Shout if
you will, but that just won't do / I, for one, would rather follow softer options')
are compatibly tear-jerking and classy. Shamefully, all of that is essentially
ruined when the piece transforms into a peppy hurdle of clichéd casings
whose stilted percussion and kitschy guitar and keyboard tones conjure every
inspirational movie montage of the 1980s. It's all well executed – and Anderson
withstands with effective credibility – but that doesn't prevent the lameness on
top from overshadowing the earnestness inside.

'Slow Marching Band' (Anderson)
A companion piece to the prior track, 'Slow Marching Band' is, at first glance,
about the end of a romantic partnership, yet directives like 'Take a hand and
take a bow / You played for me; that's all for now' seemingly suggest to the
recent loss of key associates, too. In any case, it's a poignant piano ode (with
fitting militaristic drumming) that'd risk corny banality if it weren't for the
vibrant conviction in Anderson's voice.

'Broadsword' (Anderson)
Easily one of the sturdiest inclusions, its historical setting 'about a man's
responsibility to protect the family unit' from tribal invasion is showcased
healthily by both its perilously triumphant instrumentation and heroic

proclamations. Explicitly, Anderson belts out, 'Put our backs to the north wind / Hold fast by the river / Sweet memories to drive us on for the motherland' with believable agency while the rest of the team constructs a feudal call-to-action – amplified by a legendary guitar solo and a pervading synth overcast – that epically lives up to McCaig illustrations. (It was even covered by folk metal band Turisas on 2011's *Stand up and Fight*.).

'Pussy Willow' (Anderson)
Aside from an insipid chorus – which is still passable because of Anderson's excellent recital and the verve of Pegg, Conway, and Barre – 'Pussy Willow' is downright enchanting. Its delicate and fantastical arrangement is as enrapturing as Anderson's simultaneous storytelling (concerning a girl who 'waits in her castle of make-believe / For her white knight to appear'). Most notably, the piano and keyboard touches are hugely adept at catching abandonment within their fairy-tale magic, making them the most musically attractive elements on all of *The Broadsword and the Beast*.

'Watching Me, Watching You' (Anderson)
Its programmed launching point is eerily similar to parts of Mike Oldfield's Tubular Bells, and its digitised drums deem it instantly archaic. Regrettably, that antiseptic nature also saturates the melodies and lyrics (whose retorts to 'the claustrophobic feeling of being watched all the time' as a celebrity are neither thought-provoking nor appealing). Although they'd had ups and downs before, Jethro Tull hit a new low with this autopiloted filler.

'Seal Driver' (Anderson)
Anderson's sensitive clamours and the general dynamism of the band reinstate curiosity to this otherwise run-of-the-mill dirge. Put another way, no one portion is categorically outstanding, yet the mutability of its multifaceted flow – including a moment or two for each member to seize the spotlight – allows enough coherent diversity to keep your attention. To its credit, the compromise between standard rock stylings and contemporary synthetic trappings is commendable as well.

'Cheerio' (Anderson)
As a brief gust of imperial heavenliness, it obliges *The Broadsword and the Beast* – and virtually every concert that followed for over a decade – as a golden exodus. Saintly harmonies ease with a comforting send-off ('Along the coast road / By the headland, the early lights of winter glow / I'll pour a cup to you, my darling / And raise it up, say, "Cheerio"') amongst a soothing air that's capped off by an amiable woodwind coda. One wonders how magnificent it could've been as a more developed closer, but it's nevertheless endearing and suitable as is.

Bonuses

The latest remaster of the album comes only with an additional handful of tracks. Of those, the real jewels are the pastoral and intricate 'Jack Frost and the Hooded Crow' (which could've been an outtake from *Songs from the Wood*) and the fanciful and festive 'Mayhem Maybe'. It's odd that other session recordings, such as 'The Curse', 'No Step', and 'Drive on the Young Side of Life', are absent, but they did appear elsewhere (on 1993's *Nightcap: The Unreleased Masters 1973 – 1991*). Hopefully, *The Broadsword and the Beast* will receive a more in-depth anniversary treatment when the time is right.

Under Wraps (1984)

Personnel:
Ian Anderson: vocals, acoustic guitar, drum programming, flute, Fairlight CMI
Martin Barre: electric guitar
Dave Pegg: electric bass, acoustic bass
Peter-John Vettese: keyboards, electronic programming
Trevor Key: cover photo, photography
Sheila Rock: photography
John Pasche : artwork, cover design
Produced at Ian Anderson's home studio, United Kingdom, Spring 1984 by
Ian Anderson
UK and US release date: September 1984
Highest chart places: UK: 18, USA: 76
Running time: 43:13 (Vinyl), 60:33 (CD)
Current edition: Parlophone 2005 CD remastered

By 1984, electronic music was just about fully imbued into mainstream culture, leading many artists – including progressive rock royalty like Yes, Genesis, ELP, Gentle Giant, and King Crimson – to forgo their most unique and idolised traits in the transition (to varying degrees). Although the rage of synths, digital drums, streamlined structures, and miscellaneous bizarre effects worked well for many musicians then (like David Bowie, Thomas Dolby, Kate Bush, Eurythmics, and Brian Eno) – and the style has seen a robust resurgence in recent years – it left many groups nearly unrecognisable in the homogenisation. Sadly, Jethro Tull's *Under Wraps* is one of the most egregious victims of the trend. True, they'd been dipping their feet into that pool more and more since *Stormwatch*, but it wasn't until *Under Wraps* that they became wholly submerged in it, burying the skeleton of their former glory below a vapid and trite experimental plot of meagre songwriting and hoary sounds. Today, that antediluvian triviality makes it almost ubiquitously unbearable.

As much as its precursors foreshadowed its direction, the biggest clue came in the interim, with Anderson's 1983 debut album, *Walk into Light* (which we'll get to briefly soon). More of an equal partnership with Vettese than anything, it found the pair further embracing such cutting-edge technologies and templates. Naturally, this led to *Under Wraps* being a more collaborative album with even Barre helping pen a couple of tracks. Arguably, Anderson hadn't been so hands-off since *This Was*. Likewise, it's conceivable that Anderson would've continued with programmed drums even if Conway hadn't left after the *Broadsword and the Beast* tour.

There are a few other tidbits to mention, such as that *Under Wraps* wears Anderson's 'love of espionage fiction' on its sleeve (resulting in some of its better moments, if only by default). Also, it was the first Jethro Tull album to have additional tracks included on the cassette and CD releases – which will be covered in the Bonuses section – than on the standard vinyl version.

Lastly, the ensuing concert cycle (featuring a real percussionist, Doane Perry) is often compared to that of Thick as a Brick in that 'the roadies appeared onstage, sweeping the floor, counting the audience and studying the place. All band members and instruments were covered in 'wraps', with Anderson then releasing them and the music starting'.

Over the years, the record has gained substantial apologists and appreciators, yet even Pegg has said that 'the tracks cut from *Broadsword and the Beast* would have made a better album'. As for Anderson, he confesses that while the drum machine 'annoys [him] to this day, and the public didn't like it either', he's 'glad he did it', concluding that 'it's arguably the one album where I really pushed myself as a vocalist'. In that spirit, *Under Wraps* is best viewed as an experimental product of its time that inevitably sparks cognitive dissonance in devotees. On the one hand, Jethro Tull pushed themselves into new territory (as all artists should) while adhering to the changes of the culture; however, it was their most radical and damaging mutation thus far, so that objective laudability can't make up for the subjective lambasting that the final creation deserves. As with *Too Old to Rock 'n' Roll: Too Young to Die!* and *War Child*, though, *Under Wraps*' trough would give way to 'a crest' of greater form afterwards.

'Lap of Luxury' (Anderson)
It's the first single from *Under Wraps*, and it promptly fits into the zeitgeist with its automatic percussion, feathery electric guitar tone, and cheesy punch-in affectations. Beneath all of that, it's a decent indictment of capitalism and greed ('I need money, now, to soothe my heart! / Buy me a Datsun or Toyota / Get the tax man to agree') that, like much of *Under Wraps*, would be fine for a band that hadn't proven capable of so much more in their younger days.

'Under Wraps #1' (Anderson)
The white-knuckle synth fervour of Thomas Dolby coats every element on this second single, and while it undoubtedly works better for him than it does for Jethro Tull, the song is at least moderately enjoyable once you give in to its panache. There's an overriding sense of exhilaration to its subtle spy chronicle ('Keep it quiet (go slow) / Circulate / Need to know / Stamp the date upon your file / Masquerade but well worthwhile'), and to his credit, Anderson does sing with impressive, many-sided theatricality. The chorus is a bit of an earworm, too, I'll admit.

'European Legacy' (Anderson)
'European Legacy' is the best of the introductory tracks on *Under Wraps* because it feels the most real and full-bodied (although it's still a far cry from the depth of their best efforts), with nice guitar and flute passages complementing fetching beachside verses. It also goes through a fair amount of inventive swings, and the electronic components are quirky yet reserved enough to support – rather than supersede – the clandestine draw of the

foundation. It's a song worthy of a better rendition, yes, but the one it gets here is okay, all things measured.

'Later, That Same Evening' (Anderson, Vettese)

Appearing like the sequel to 'European Legacy', it's a sparser and darker continuation of the sordid reconnaissance between a male narrator and a woman with whom he shared a 'a drink or four' before she escaped in a submarine after hearing an 'early warning from a hidden phone'. The anguished strings and piano notes help make Anderson's tale of a fleeting fling without closure more captivating, yet it's another instance of a potentially great song partially being squandered by dated production and lacklustre instrumentation. It's a highlight of *Under Wraps*, no doubt, but it could've been so much more if granted lusher attention.

'Saboteur' (Anderson, Vettese)

Ironically, 'Saboteur' sabotages the upward trajectory of the last two pieces by being an exclusively unexceptional and gimmicky entry with little to latch onto. There is a lot going on in terms of melding feisty rock and electronic timbres, but it's a disorderly and disorienting mess whose vocals fail to salvage the wreck. Even its lyrics –usually a saving grace in those rare times when nothing else really appeals – are relatively clunky ('Painted ducks across your landscape / Happy in your domesticity (it don't come free) / Misfortune, like a sparrow hawk, hangs over you').

'Radio Free Moscow' (Anderson, Vettese)

The neighbouring voiceovers are an operative way of legitimatising the espionage lore, but apart from that, 'Radio Free Moscow' is incessantly ho-hum and hackneyed. It's among the most severe cases of the contrived 1980s polish on *Under Wraps* (although the acoustic respite near the end is good as an isolated section), and while Anderson's performance is empirically solid, what he's singing isn't very engaging.

'Nobody's Car' (Anderson, Vettese, Barre)

Like 'Radio Free Moscow' and 'European Legacy', there's a tropical breeziness to it, and the horns are surely a distinguishing ingredient. Outside of that and the further emphasising of Anderson's increasingly transparent interest in automobiles (used here to frame another spy thriller snapshot), there's not much to save it from being deplorable in its cringe-worthy mediocrity. Frankly, it's utterly baffling how lazy and ordinary 'Nobody's Car' is considering that it has three members behind the writing wheel.

'Heat' (Anderson, Vettese)

The wistful woodwinds and piano that kick this one off have promise (despite being juxtaposed by more programmed drums), but as usual, that's misspent alongside other irksome new wave permutations (no matter how well they're played). Surprisingly, it's Anderson's lifeless verses and horrid belches of 'Get out of the heat' that take 'Heat' from merely dull to downright intolerable. It's another nail in the coffin of cementing *Under Wraps* as a huge misfire in the Jethro Tull canon.

'Under Wraps #2' (Anderson)
Its acoustic majesty unequivocally outshines the earlier variation, recalling the splendours of similar compositions from the 1970s and doing justice to the heartfelt core. The harmonies and strums are thoroughly idyllic, the episodic tambourine hits are always advantageous, and Pegg's bass adds a rustic and weighty lower end that's right at home. The only downside is that it makes you yearn for a stripped-down take on some of the other pieces since they'd surely be easier to appreciate when unburdened by their synthesised shackles.

'Paparazzi' (Anderson, Vettese, Barre)
Its undying social commentary notwithstanding ('They've got their crayons out / To colour in the book / Snap it up, flash away / Steal a camel for a day'), 'Paparazzi' is another superficial poppy trudge that, in many ways, is the antithesis of what Jethro Tull carved out as their niche way back when. It's perpetually machinelike and dumbed down, with Barre outwardly neutered in implementing purely serviceable skill.

'Apogee' (Anderson, Vettese)
Under Wraps wraps up with another antiseptic number that touches upon another one of the group's most common topics: aerial exploration. Air traffic reports (and the like) are interwoven within the electric guitar jabs, metallic syncopation, periodic keyboard flare-ups, and brooding synths that cascade around Anderson's passionate but unmelodic reading. Try as they might, it's a tepid and artificial closer that paradoxically feels like the only logical way to go out given the course of such qualities across the whole LP.

Bonuses
Mercifully, the 2005 CD comprises just a video for 'Lap of Luxury' – in which Anderson is chauffeured around town and then chased by the band as debonair sycophants – and the four tracks from the original cassette release ('General Crossing', 'Astronomy', 'Tundra', and 'Automotive Engineering'). All but 'General Crossing' also appeared on the 'Lap of Luxury' 12-inch, and of the supplementary set, 'Tundra' is the least offensive due to having fewer antiquated peculiarities and a marginally tuneful score. Mostly, they just reaffirm *Under Wraps'* problems.

Crest of a Knave (1987)

Personnel:

Ian Anderson: vocals, acoustic guitar, electric guitar, additional percussion, keyboards, Synclavier, drum
 programming (1, 5, 9)
Martin Barre: electric guitar, acoustic guitar
Dave Pegg: electric bass, acoustic bass (4)
Doane Perry: drums, percussion (2, 7)
Gerry Conway: drums, percussion (3, 4, 6, 8)
Ric Sanders: violin (6)
Robin Black: engineer
Tim Matyear: engineer
Stephen W. Tayler: engineer, remixing
John Pasche: art direction
Martyn Goddard: photography
Andrew Jamieson: artwork, calligraphy
Produced at Black Barn Studio, London, Early 1987 by Ian Anderson
UK and US release date: September 1987
Highest chart places: UK: 19, USA: 32
Running time: 39:30 (Vinyl), 48:50 (CD)
Current edition: Parlophone 2005 CD remastered

Jethro Tull took synth rock as far as they could with *Under Wraps* – to understandably sour results and reception – so it's quite good that Crest of a Knave signifies an updated return to form. There are electronic dabs here and there, but they never blemish the music; instead, they act as faint and appropriate glimpses of former gaudiness in the midst of Anderson and crew charging full force with a reconciliation of both modernised and trademark styles. Hence, the record marks yet another new chapter for the ensemble that, even with its proclivity for unvaried AOR over progressive and folk rock, manages a sustaining and welcomed recovery (in more ways than one).

As mentioned previously, Anderson respects Under Wraps for pushing his vocals farther than ever before, which makes the subsequent throat infection he suffered while on tour poetically disastrous since it's a major reason for why he sounds so startlingly different on *Crest of a Knave* (plus why it took so long for the album to arrive). He elaborates: 'I ripped up my throat – I couldn't sing and I thought maybe time was up and I'd blown my voice completely. I spent a year not doing anything but seeing throat specialists, so it wasn't until the summer of '86 that we went out and did some shows'. As common a comparison as it is, linking this rendering of Jethro Tull to bands like Dire Straits is unavoidable.

Although he was on stage for those summer shows, Vettese was no longer a member after the hiatus (no doubt due to Anderson's need for a stylistic rebirth, as well as Vettese's desire to have a fruitful path as a songwriter, producer, and arranger, which he did). Aiding the official trio of Anderson, Barre, and Pegg (who 'purposefully [wrote] songs in a lower key' to assist Anderson's voice) was Doane Perry, *The Broadsword and the Beast* drummer Gerry Conway, and Fairport Convention violinist Ric Sanders (further cementing the relationship between the two bands, coincidental or not). Robin Black returned too – alongside other engineers – to guarantee proper production. Along those lines, Barre says, 'That's the album where a lot of things were of my invention. There are still chunks of the music where Ian very much knew what he wanted, but I think my input was far greater on that album than on any other'. In many ways, then, *Crest of a Knave* is designed as the anti-*Under Wraps*.

The difference between the two was so great that *Crest of a Knave* won the 1989 Grammy Award for Best Hard Rock/Metal Performance Vocal or Instrumental, beating out frontrunners ...*And Justice for All* (Metallica) and *Nothing's Shocking* (Jane's Addiction). Widely considered a career-spanning token of recognition rather than a prize for the collection itself, this turn of events nonetheless still dumbfounds countless people. In fact, Jethro Tull didn't even show up to the ceremony because the odds were stacked so highly against them, and Chrysalis quickly took out an advert congratulating them with this copy: 'The flute is a [heavy] metal instrument!' In 2007, Entertainment Weekly called it one of the biggest upsets in Grammy history, and in 2014, Rolling Stone's Andy Greene listed it as the 18th 'Most Awesomely Retro Moments in Grammy History', aptly surmising that 'the Grammys have never quite gotten over this embarrassment'.

Beyond that controversy, the LP earned mixed to positive reactions from critics and patrons who consistently took Anderson to task for jumping on musical bandwagons but at least appreciated its the aforementioned turn toward a more habituated sound. It also led to a pick-up of popularity on radio and television (especially MTV). Chart-wise, it basically landed alongside *Under Wraps* in the UK, yet it did far better in America and earned Gold certification in both places. In retrospect, *Crest of a Knave* receives a bit more reverence than it warrants for eschewing the electronic disadvantages of its forebear and for being a comeback of sorts, but that doesn't mean it's not an admirable part of the catalogue.

'Steel Monkey' (Anderson)
The sequencer at the start seems like a figurative transition between early and late '80s Jethro Tull, and it's employed healthily within the crushing rhythms and guitar riffs that follow. Of course, Anderson's nasally new timbre is startling at first – and it's at its most pronounced here – yet his enigmatic personification of high-rise steel construction workers ('Some look up and some look down / From three hundred feet above the ground') eventually becomes accustomed and, well, fun. Barre's intervallic licks add spiciness to strengthen the song's declaration that while the Jethro Tull of yesteryear is gone, this simplified new one can hold its own in the current scene.

'Farm on the Freeway' (Anderson)

A tragic account of a farmer losing his land due to eminent domain, its mellowly dejected flute, piano, guitar, and bass interactions immediately take you back to classic Jethro Tull. Similarly, Anderson reiterates his model knack for moving lyricism and convincing deliveries in richly describing a father and son saying goodbye to 'good shelter down there ... where the sweet stream run' and being left with only 'a cheque and a pickup truck'. Logically, it gets more penetrating as it goes, with Barre and Anderson uniting instrumentally like old times before reprising the inaugural arrangement (as Jethro Tull often does) and ending with a haunting outro of flute and electric guitar screeches. Honestly, Anderson's altered voice is the only thing that would stop it from being passed off as a shelved composition from ten years prior.

'Jump Start' (Anderson)

Its catchy and unassuming acoustic presence (with woodwind eruptions, as you'd expect) also harkens back to greater periods, as do the power-driven blocks built around a hook that amends slightly after each stanza ('Hey, ____, won't you come on over / Hook me up to the power lines of your love / Jumpstart, or tow me away'). Halfway in, they let loose in ways they haven't for years, with Pegg and Conway dexterously holding firm around Barre and Anderson's freak-outs. From start to end, it's an awesome ebb and flow of temperaments that makes you glad to have vintage Jethro Tull back again (for all intents and purposes). Like much of *Crest of a Knave*, the songwriting may not be consistently remarkable but the players absolutely soar with rejuvenated appetite.

'She Said She Was a Dancer' (Anderson)

'She Said She Was a Dancer' carries on Anderson's fondness for writing about unrequited or perilous dealings with foreign or mysterious women (in this case, 'Miss Moscow', who 'spoke in riddles while the vodka listened'). Upfront, Pegg's acoustic bass plucks foil the disjointed electric guitar arcs (which kind of evoke the beginning of 'Baker Street Muse') smoothly; once the stylish percussion and vocals come in, you can't help but think of Mark Knopfler's laidback assertions atop the cool slickness of his most iconic group. There's not much more to it than that (or at all), and even with some humiliatingly pedestrian language ('I'm your Pepsi-Cola / But you won't take me out the can'), it's harmless and hip enough.

'Budapest' (Anderson)

Written 'in a hotel the morning after a show [in 1986], about the vision of some slender and tall athletic creature who was serving sandwiches backstage', 'Budapest' (which was originally twice as lengthy) is the standout of *Crest of a Knave*, and for good reason. As Anderson puts it, 'it embodies a lot of different nuances ... from classical to slightly bluesy to folk, and it just slips between them and you don't see the stitching'. The tasteful compunction of its early piano, flute, synth, and acoustic guitar jumble bids a beautiful prelude to the matter-of-fact ballad, and it intensifies around that edifice with sultry valour toward a lively middle full of nostalgic textural trade-offs. After another two verses, a more calculated drama coalesces when those same tools entangle and mimic each other as they approach the climax. It's an endlessly hypnotic parade of how much resourceful technique Jethro Tull still possessed.

'Mountain Men' (Anderson)

Melodically and lyrically, the first line must consciously allude to the 'poet and the painter' part of *Thick as a Brick*. Its starry chirps and echoed woodwinds yield a chilling mood to offset the scorching backdrop of Anderson's testament to the harrows of the war ('I did all they asked of me / Died in the trenches and at Alamein / Died in the Falklands on TV'). It's an arresting track sonically and conceptually, with hefty pathos and amendments that never loosen their grip.

'Raising Steam' (Anderson)

To be blunt, 'Raising Steam' is a by-the-numbers hard rocker about working-class escapism that leaves much to be desired (especially after the sophistication and scope of 'Budapest' and 'Mountain Men'). I suppose the digital decorations add intriguing flamboyance to this base level anthem, but even that's a stretch. Hyperbolic or not, I imagine that it took about as long to create as it does to say its title.

Bonuses and contemporary tracks

Coronach (Palmer)

'Coronach' was credited to Palmer and Jethro Tull and used for the Channel 4 programme *The Blood of the British,* so was also released as a single in the UK. On its own, the piece is, well, peacefully empty and slow, with Anderson's drawn-out verses providing comforting narrations filled with evocative descriptions ('Brown furrow shine / Beneath the rain washed blue'). Around him, mild timbres (mostly acoustic guitar, horns, drums, and harp) glide around his recollections and aid in constructing an enticingly epic but gentle environment.

'Part of the Machine' (Anderson)

A typical whirlwind of electric and acoustic oscillations, this entry evokes the sea instantly with its breezy, high-pitched flute and acoustic guitar passages. Afterwards, Anderson's slightly strained vocals effectually offer matter-of-fact authority within the confines of the arrangement (which is satisfying but unremarkable aside from its midsection influx of intricately stacked instrumentation). In other words, it's a strong rock song by conventional standards but only an average Jethro Tull venture.

Crest of a Knave's most up-to-date release offers just three more selections: 'Dogs in the Midwinter' and 'The Walking Edge' (both of which were on the original CD), plus 'Part of the Machine' (originally on 1988's *20 Years of Jethro Tull* three-disc boxset). The former is pleasantly punchy, while the second is meditative and roomy. All three tracks enhance what's already an agreeable record without bringing anything amazing to the table.

Rock Island (1989)

Personnel:
Ian Anderson: vocals, acoustic guitar, Synclavier, flute, keyboards, mandolin, drums, percussion (2, 7)
Martin Barre: electric guitar, acoustic guitar
Dave Pegg: electric bass, acoustic bass, mandolin
Doane Perry: drums, percussion
Maartin Allcock: keyboards (1, 10)
Peter-John Vettese: additional keyboards (3, 4, 5, 6)
John Pasche: art direction
Anton Morris: illustrations
Jim Gibson: illustrations
Martyn Goddard: photography
Tim Matyear: mixing
Mark Tucker: assistant mixing
Produced at Ian Anderson and Dave Pegg's home studios, United Kingdom, Early 1989 by Ian Anderson
UK and US release date: August 1989
Highest chart places: UK: 18, USA: 56
Running time: 50:21
Current edition: Parlophone 2006 CD remastered

Appraised by Anderson as 'the antidote to the more cheerful *Crest of a Knave*' because of its 'mostly dark subject matter of alienation and desolation', Jethro Tull's 17th studio undertaking, *Rock Island*, is a noticeably heavier stylistic sibling. According to Jon Hotten in 'Every Jethro Tull Album Ranked Worst to Best', it was partially written in the Isle of Skye in Scotland. Now an official quartet (Anderson, Barre, Pegg, and Perry, in his first complete studio recording as a member), the band also brought back Vettese – as well as another Fairport Convention participant, Maartin Allcock – to handle most of the keyboard duties.

Reportedly, they'd planned to include reoccurring themes but, save for a couple of light instances, ultimately didn't. Also, 80% of it was written in less than two weeks and then quickly and congenially laid down. Anderson explicates:

> *I just stick to a schedule ... that will facilitate a focused release. Putting yourself in a position where you have to produce is an excellent way to get the creative juices flowing again. If I know I have ten days before the guys are due to arrive to record, it puts the pressure on me to produce. I like it that way ... Jethro Tull is, from time to time, an extraordinarily democratic band in the sense that there is a lot of cooperative musical involvement ... I may have written most of the songs as original sketches, but the way they come out can change dramatically.*

Looking back, he infers that *Rock Island* 'missed out on having some humour elements ... [it] had two or three songs that were just a little too serious'. Yet, it benefited from the peak in popularity generated by *Crest of a Knave* to harvest the troupe another Gold record in the UK (as well as a successful tour in which 'silhouettes of lithe dancers' were projected during 'Kissing Willie', 'ending with an image that bordered on pornographic'). Overall, *Rock Island* is a more stable and characteristic album than its predecessor – it doesn't have as drastic a divide between highs and lows, nor is it as derivative since everyone was better settled into their roles – so it works well as a valediction to the decade before the rise of the 1990s.

'Kissing Willie' (Anderson)
'Kissing Willie' was first released as a popular single in 1988 (alongside a Storm Thorgerson video set in the Georgian era that, Anderson laments, depicts 'an all-too-regrettable, unsubtle piece of saucy innuendo' that 'Benny Hill would have been proud of'). The rhythmically irregular fury of flute, electric guitar, and piano that runs throughout is borderline folk metal, and Anderson is more like his old self as he bemoans a woman he likes kissing his best friend. True, the femme fatale aspect ('Nice girl but a bad girl's better / Qualifies in both ways to my mind') preserves Anderson's penchant for philandering narrators and isn't exactly pro-feminist (especially by 2019 standards), but he's right in upholding it as 'good fun' even if it's 'not a great song'. Perry trims with subtle flair, too, and Barre still finds stimulating fills amidst the frolicking, solidifying it as an invigorating opener.

'The Rattlesnake Trail' (Anderson)
Commonly thought to be about a somewhat destitute person reaching for a better life (no matter the cost), the wah-wah riffs, light keyboard knick-knacks, and alternating percussion make it more pleasing than it would be otherwise. Even so, it's fairly average, and Anderson's snaky singing doesn't do it any favours.

'Ears of Tin' (Anderson)
Its misty-eyed verses ('In the last hours of a sunset rendezvous / Chill breeze against the tide that carries me from you') and parallel arrangement are introspectively tender (especially the mandolin and woodwind mimicry and earthly keyboard drops). The impassioned chorus and bridge are nice contrasts, too, and augment the bittersweet romantic callback afterwards. All in all, it's a successfully diverse and beguiling apposition of contentment on the Isle of Skye versus isolation in the city (hence the original title, 'The Mainland Blues').

'Undressed to Kill' (Anderson)
Like many Jethro Tull tracks of the time, 'Undressed to Kill' is performed skilfully and fills the silence fine, but it's nothing more than that, disappointingly enough.

It's another ode to a prostitute with suggestive puns – 'Find some place to touch down / Find a landing strip' and 'I wait outside, my motor running / I've got a warm dream to unload', unless I'm the one with a dirty mind – that doesn't strive to be more than a superficial placeholder. Rather than exude singularity (outside of the token timbres), it's a mindless and middling time that countless other acts could have come up with.

'Rock Island' (Anderson)
This one mirrors the isolation leitmotif and heavenly ambience from 'Ears of Tin', with Pegg and Perry serving as the steadfast guiding lights that steer Anderson's verbal and instrumental quips. There's an even larger range and balance between the lenient and forceful gradations, however, and a prevailing stateliness around Anderson's regretful returns to 'Rock Island'. The obligatory midway jam is, well, compulsory and familiar, but it does allow Pegg, in particular, to stand out with some tricky zig-zags. It's not their best title track, of course, but it's certainly not their worst, either.

'Heavy Water' (Anderson)
The other single put out the year before the album, it is among the catchiest songs on *Rock Island*. In Barbara Espinoza's book *Driving in Diverse: A Collective Profile of Jethro Tull*, Anderson divulges that it's based on one of his earliest trips to New York City: 'It was really, really hot and uncomfortable. Suddenly, blessed rain! I was standing out there getting wet and walking down the street; everybody else was running away from the rain. I realised that each drop of rain that had fallen on me made a dirty black mark. It was raining coal and sulphur'. That desperation and disgust come through in the rugged vocals and straightforward music (that's peppered with dainty tracings to keep the momentum going).

'Another Christmas Song' (Anderson)
Despite its theoretically cynical self-aware title (it's really just a reference to the much earlier 'Christmas Song'), 'Another Christmas Song' is actually quite a heart-warming tale of an elderly man thinking about his children and hoping that everyone else is 'connected to that long-distance phone'. It's charming to hear Anderson sing so genuinely about a universal (and secular) purpose for Christmas: taking time out to cherish and nurture the bonds you have with people in the face of so much surrounding internal and external conflicts, including 'talks of origins and cultural identity'. Barre adds little touches in-between the celebratory woodwinds and pounding drums to personify the soul of the season further, making it lovely in sound and spirit alike.

'The Whaler's Dues' (Anderson)
It's the most epic piece on *Rock Island*, with a despairingly enticing array of tones (woodwinds, high-pitched keyboard, gentle cymbal taps) at the top that

conjure the intro of 'Pibroch (Cup in Hand)' from *Songs from the Wood*. It upholds this environment as Anderson bellows about how 'money speaks' and 'soft hearts lose' when men on the sea do bad things. Smartly, it gets fiercer whenever he asks for forgiveness – and is met with a dense 'No!' each time – to achieve an affectingly fatalistic and engrossingly cold showcase of how effectively the group could still breathe cinematic life into their storytelling.

'Big Riff and Mando' (Anderson)

This second-to-last outing 'reflects life on the road for the relentlessly touring musicians, giving a wry account of the theft of Barre's prized mandolin by a stage-struck fan'. Its tongue-in-cheek frankness ('Big Riff, rough boy / Wants to be a singer in a band / A little slow in the brain box / But he had a quick right hand') is matched by surprisingly delicate and touching instrumentation in-between the hard rock upsurges. Anderson's flute upswings are ceaselessly spectacular, too, and Perry undoubtedly does some of his most difficult playing of the whole collection. In a way, it's like *Thick as a Brick* in that the execution is far more rewarding and committed than the concept.

'Strange Avenues' (Anderson)

Another moody beginning – unbalanced acoustic guitar, woodwind, and bass notes dancing around infrequent percussive and piano interruptions – gives way to chaos before being quelled for a transformative and sombre nod to *Aqualung* ('The wino sleeps / Cold coat lined with the money section / Looking like a record cover / From 1971'). The off-kilter and bi-polar phrasing of every component lingers long after Anderson heads out 'from your rock island' (a clever bit of continuity) and hears 'a young girl whisper / "Are you ever lonely, just like me?"' Like 'And Further On' from *A*, it's cryptic, abstract, and deceptively simple, leaving you dumbfounded by, yet infatuated with, what it all means.

Bonuses

Recorded live in Zurich, Switzerland on October 13, 1989, the trio of extras – 'Christmas Song,' 'Cheap Day Return/Mother Goose', and 'Locomotive Breath' – were originally released on the UK CD single of 'Another Christmas Song'. They're all relatively faithful (although 'Mother Goose' is also just a solo acoustic performance) aside from Anderson's voice, yet there's surely more content hidden away in the annals (to hopefully be featured on an expanded anniversary edition).

Catfish Rising (1991)

Personnel:
Ian Anderson: vocals, acoustic guitar, electric guitar, flute, keyboards, drums, percussion, acoustic
mandolin, electric mandolin
Martin Barre: electric guitar
Dave Pegg: electric bass, acoustic bass
Doane Perry: drums, percussion
Andrew Giddings: keyboards (1, 4, 8)
Foster Patterson: keyboards (10)
John Bundrick: keyboards (11)
Matt Pegg: bass guitar (1, 4, 7)
Scott Hunter: drums, percussion (5)
Tim Matyear: engineer
Mark Tucker: assistant engineer
Martyn Goddard: photography
John Pasche: design
Phil Rogers: design
Geoff Halpin: design (logo and monogram)
Jim Gibson: illustration
Produced at Ian Anderson and Dave Pegg's home studios, United Kingdom, Early 1991 by Ian Anderson
UK and US release date: September 1991
Highest chart places: UK: 27, USA: 88
Running time: 42:49 (Vinyl), 60:24 (CD)
Current edition: Parlophone 2006 CD remastered

Unfortunately, there's not much to say about the context and background of *Catfish Rising*. It's the debut of keyboardist Andrew Giddings and is more or less a bluesier companion to *Rock Island*. Thankfully, they didn't try to adapt to the flavour of the time – as they had in the early 1980s – by taking on the burgeoning grunge scene set by Pearl Jam, Nirvana, Soundgarden, and Alice in Chains. In fact – and as Rabey points out – 'the music [was] played on instruments that originated from trees' to 'return to the blues roots of *This Was* over 20 years after Anderson had moved on and "progressed". The result was that fans didn't quite know what to make of the album – they either loved it or hated it'. Anderson concurs in saying that it wasn't the most 'fashionable' record to release before joking that *Catfish Rising*'s biggest sin is its album cover: 'Too much black! Too much Spinal! No space to sign autographs with a black Sharpie'. Its relatively disappointing chart placements only confirmed those truths, and many fans are still divided on whether it's better or worse than *Crest of a Knave* and *Rock Island* (almost no one puts it in the middle). For my money, it's the least wide-ranging and attractive of the three but it's not a total washout, and it makes the consequent return to different roots look better by comparison.

'This Is Not Love' (Anderson)

Melodically, this opener almost like a colder and more condensed variant of 'Heavy Water' from Rock Island. For the most part, it's a totally listenable but nondescript and mildly repetitive track about a person reflecting on better times ('Sunburst images of summers gone / Think I see us in these promenade days / Before we learned October's song') as their relationship comes to its end. It leans toward being uninspired AOR at times – and Anderson's periodic yowls are uncharacteristic and irritating – but it's okay in and of itself. The brief start-and-stop break and ensuing guitar solo about two minutes in, elevating it a tad, too.

'Occasional Demons' (Anderson)

Despite its robotic drumming, its leisurely pace and relentless juxtaposition of electric and acoustic guitar licks sufficiently hold your attention. Pegg and Anderson include some instrumental garnishes, too, and the use of animals as metaphors ('We're all kinds of animals coming here / Occasional demons, too' and 'Mmmm, you see those snakes that crawl / They're just dying to trip you up') does evoke the *War Child* and Château d'Hérouville projects (if only by an unintentional hair). By and large, 'Occasional Demons' is a humdrum rocker done with great precision.

'Rocks on the Road' (Anderson)

Acoustic fingerpicking and solemn slice-of-life observations instantly allure, with lines like 'Down in the half-lit bar of the hotel / There's a call for the last round of the day / Push back the stool, take that elevator ride / Fall in bed and kick my shoes away') – alongside comments about shower, plumbing, and city noise woes. This brings to life Anderson's weary role as a travelling salesman of sorts. This foundation is also maturely developed with elegant pathos by piano, flute, percussion, strings, mandolin, electric guitar and bass toward a jazzy break and poignantly successive resolution home. As a result, it hovers above pretty much everything else on *Catfish Rising*.

'Thinking Round Corners' (Anderson)

A nonsensical and raucous entry perfect for drunken Mississippi square dances, 'Thinking Round Corners' clearly calls back to Jethro Tull's earliest days in its slide guitar, shuffling rhythms, and woodwind motif. All of that would be a passable way to spend the time if not for Anderson's annoying vocal artifices. Sure, they fit the homage intention and add personality to the track, but that doesn't assuage how much of its forced awkwardness is a turnoff.

'Still Loving You Tonight' (Anderson)

'Still Loving You Tonight' is a patient blues waltz at heart. It has all the requisite appurtenances, such as six-string wails, dim syncopation, and grief-stricken yet self-assured speeches ('You want to know how I can leave you? / How can I move along this way? / Too much of a good thing can make you crazy / And it's a good thing that happened to me today'). In addition, the underlying organ provides an extra layer of emotion, and in general, it's an adroit rendering of a standard genre tune.

'Doctor to My Disease' (Anderson)
A more victorious and energetic cohort to the prior dirge on coupling, this side two starter winningly barrels onward thanks to a thunderous and bustling interplay between Barre and Pegg. As usual, the former never lets up with his piercing accentuations, whereas the latter moves along like a heated locomotive. No doubt, the others satisfy as well, but it's the guitar duo that boosts it most (especially since lyrics like 'Well, you put my heart in overdrive / Hand me the bullet I must bite' exemplify the lame lethargy in Anderson's symbolic language around that time).

'Like a Tall Thin Girl' (Anderson)
Encouraged by Perry's interest in an Indian restaurant waitress on Baker Street during the *Under Wraps* tour, this acoustic arrangement has some enchanting and appropriate cultural accessories. However, whatever carefree fanciness it offers is almost entirely undermined by Anderson's blatantly sleazy wingman perversions ('Big boy, Doane, he's a drummer ... stands six foot three in his underwear / Going to get him down here and see / If this good lady's got a little sister 'bout the same size as me') and inexorable pursuit ('She looked like a tall thin girl / Well, can I fetch for it? / Well, maybe I can stretch for it? / Well, am I up for it? / Or do I have to go down for it?'). It's not an outright chronicle of two middle-aged men as sexual predators, yet it comes too close to look past for its marginal pros.

'Sparrow on the Schoolyard Wall' (Anderson)
Luckily, this one restores some merit with its inspirational message about blossoming out of your shell as a nebbish intellectual and becoming a social creature who 'should be ranging down the freeway / With some friends from the mall'. Perry and Pegg play it cool as Giddings, Anderson, and Barre strike up an even dynamic from start to end; it's not creatively novel or challenging, but it does permeate affable refinement all the same.

'Roll Yer Own' (Anderson)
In a July 1991 interview with Gloria Hunniford for BBC Radio 2, Anderson was pressed to explain that the penultimate 'Roll Yer Own' is not about drugs (as Chrysalis suspected), but instead about 'an intrinsically sexual nature, and really more to do with ... female masturbation'. It's no wonder, then, what he means by 'Roll yer own / If you can't buy readymade' and 'If you don't get

enough of that electric love / Don't try to get by / Roll yer own'. The scarce
blues backing – with walking bass, hand claps, and down-home guitarwork
– does little more than make it musical, so there's not much to its bland but
slightly amusing and progressive runtime.

'Gold-Tipped Boots, Black Jacket and Tie' (Anderson)

Another acoustic romp (see: the erstwhile suggested lack of assortment on
Catfish Rising), it centres on reinvention and empowerment after feeling like a
'has-been' who's 'battered and bruised'. It's countrified and playful – with the
élan of an impeccably rehearsed jug band on the porch of a Southern bar or
corner store – but, as with much of the LP, it's a one trick pony with only a half-
decent, and very familiar, illusion.

Bonuses

The newest grouping rounds up the original bonus 12-inch set ('When Jesus
Came to Play', 'Sleeping with the Dog', and 'White Innocence'), 'Night in the
Wilderness' (which was on most of the *Catfish Rising*-era singles), and a live
version of 'Jump Start' that first appeared as the B-side to 'This is Not Love'.
Curiously, 'White Innocence' and 'Sleeping with the Dog' come between 'Like
a Tall Thin Girl' and 'Gold-Tipped Boots, Black Jacket and Tie', changing the
final flow of *Catfish Rising*. As individual add-ons, each earns its place ('White
Innocence' is indubitably the strongest due to its symphonic and elaborate
versatility).

Roots to Branches (1995)

Personnel:
Ian Anderson: vocals, acoustic guitar, flute
Martin Barre: electric guitar
Dave Pegg: bass guitar (3, 5, 11)
Steve Bailey: bass guitar (1, 6, 7, 8, 9, 10)
Doane Perry: drums, percussion
Andrew Giddings: keyboards
Martyn Goddard: photography
Zarkowski Designs: artwork, design
Chris Blair: mastering
Produced at Ian Anderson's home studio, United Kingdom, December 1994 – June 1995 by Ian Anderson
UK and US release date: September 1995
Highest chart places: UK: 20, USA: 114
Running time: 60:00 (CD)
Current edition: Parlophone 2006 CD remastered

At the time of release, *Roots to Branches* marked the longest time gap between Jethro Tull studio efforts, as the group spent the immediate years after 1991's *Catfish Rising* working on multiple collections to commemorate their 25th anniversary (not to mention Anderson's second solo project, *Divinities: Twelve Dances with God*, which came out a few months beforehand). In the eyes of many devotees – myself included – this prolonged immersion into their past helped prompt a re-evaluation of what did or didn't work about their formula, leading to tried-and-true yet revitalised seeds for the new album. By no means on par with their chief works of the 1970s, *Roots to Branches* is inarguably a callback to them (with some fresh DNA to boot) and, with its reliability, erudition, appetite, and an overarching attention to detail, the best Jethro Tull album since *A*, if not earlier.

There's absolutely some of the beloved Englishness of days gone by here – and Anderson has called the LP 'the 90s version of Stand Up, because it has a lot of the things that ... represented the key elements of Jethro Tull ... lots of flute, lots of riffy guitars and quite a broad palette of influences'. But it is most fascinating in its exploration of jazz, Arabic, and Far Eastern emblems. In fact, Nollen sees it as the 'Indian *Songs from the Wood*', and while that's partially true, Roots to Branches accomplishes more than just that as a fine intermingling of progressive rock and World Music (with unremitting symphonic fixings to – at least in part – mask Anderson's naturally aged tone and limited range).

As for its line-up, *Roots to Branches* – their last effort for Chrysalis and the first to not differ between the vinyl and CD versions – introduces keyboardist Andrew Giddings as an official member. Save for a few tracks, the album also signifies Pegg's end with the band due to (as Anderson reconciles)

'the resurgent popularity of Fairport Convention – always his first love –
and the increasingly difficult task of being the bass player of two bands
at the same time'. Bassist Steve Bailey 'turned up on a freezing January
morning' to Anderson's studio to fill in, and he does an excellent job. That
inopportuneness notwithstanding, realising the project was an exciting and
fruitful process, as Perry gloats: 'There was something special about the
recording of [it] and I think we all knew that when we were doing it ... There
were some really wonderful moments'.

Critically, the record received positive but reserved reviews (around 3/5
stars, usually) in 1995; however, it's grown in popularity and appreciation ever
since, with publications like *Prog-Sphere*, *Ultimate Classic Rock*, and *Classic
Rock Magazine* placing it almost directly in the middle of their 'worst to best'
Jethro Tull spectrums. As for Anderson, he feels confident about it aside from
admitting, 'The only thing about it that lets me down is that I made it sound
a little too Seventies', as well as it sounding too much like 'live performance'
instead of a studio creation. This is a distinction that Barre actually liked since
it was a throwback to 'the early days' and moved them away from the 'jigsaw
method' of building up 'from click parts' and drum machines). Again, the
disc is far from peak Jethro Tull, but it embodies their finest hours far more
than it has any right to, and the robust inclusion of reasonably new cultural
fundamentals (that, to be fair, Anderson had been toying with since his early
20s) within that set-up is as refreshing as it is motivated. Best of all, it's a
consistent highpoint after so many mixed bags, demonstrating how much bark
Jethro Tull still had after nearly three complete decades of creativity.

'Roots to Branches' (Anderson)

Their first opening title track in almost twenty years (unless you count
1982's 'Beastie'), it roasts momentarily in its ominous stew (a buzzing guitar
theme, glistening drums, and ensnaring woodwinds) before exploding. From
there, the soft and heavy undulations of main ideas are classic Jethro Tull,
as is Anderson's theologically centred outspokenness about the twisting of
words for power ('True disciples carrying that message / To colour just a
little / With their personal touch'). It's filled with engaging modulations and
reinterpretations – including some dizzying detours and even a brief jazz
bypass – that evoke their progressive rock heyday, and Giddings proves a
priceless asset with his sundry contributions. It's a thrilling and multifaceted
ride that announces how full-bodied *Roots to Branches* will be. After all, Jethro
Tull had survived well enough through the 1980s and early 1990s, but they
hadn't sounded this ambitious, focused, and lively in quite some time.

'Rare and Precious Chain' (Anderson)

One of the last pieces composed for *Roots to Branches*, its Indian percussion,
flutes, and miscellaneous sounds imbue striking character into its rock
core. According to Perry, the song 'took off' like it 'had a life of its own',

encouraging him to apply 'part African drums and Moroccan and sort of Eastern Indian influences' to Barre's 'psychedelic 1960s' veneers, among other rudiments. In contrast to how the majority of the LP was rehearsed ahead of time and recorded live. It began as an acoustic song that then needed the other members to 'figure out what to play' over it. It's therefore ironic that the songwriting itself is essentially only a footing for the vivid experiment around it, a fusion of practices that, as Anderson wished, comes across more like 'a vigorous hybrid and not merely some disastrous genetic mix-up'. Their yearning for something eclectically ethnic and off-the-wall (but also cohesive and traditional) bleeds through each mesmerising measure.

'Out of the Noise' (Anderson)
The vigour of crisscrossing flutes and electric guitars amongst frisky rhythms and keyboard post-scripts suits the tale of a 'crazy suicide mongrel' narrowly dodging all sorts of city hazards. Even with its majorly unswerving form, 'Out of the Noise' sustains inquisitiveness because of its many minor brushstrokes (with a unified tangent from Pegg and Giddings appealing most). Anderson's voice is expressly hearty as well, so it's clear that he's as into it as the rest of the team.

'This Free Will' (Anderson)
The classical and Arabic qualities (both elusive and in-your-face) truly heighten Anderson's insularly engrossing battle between fate and destiny as he tries to reconnect with a woman he's loved since childhood (who 'can almost remember [his] name', so it's no doubt a one-sided undertaking). Barre's playing is notably dissonant and unpredictable yet proper, and the rest of the music wisely mutates to interpret Anderson's struggles. It would be captivating even if he weren't singing, so his lyrics and melodies are just the icings on the cake.

'Valley' (Anderson)
'Valley' starts with the spotlight on an enigmatic flute solo that's sporadically disrupted by a crash of drums and guitars; it then flows into a reflective acoustic pattern (with lustrous earthly appendages) as Anderson pensively tells of peaceful farming and merchant lives being turned to hate-filled bedlam 'in the long red, red valley'. Clearly, it's a song about bigotry and skirmishes, and while it's most overtly an 'anti-war song aimed at Bosnia', he – in an October 1995 interview with Gerry Galipault of the Chicago Tribune – clarifies that it applies to any situation involving people who are 'intolerant of their neighbours and jealous and suspicious, feeling that they impede each other through their proximity in some way'. Its arid waves of tranquillity and turmoil entertain as much as they elucidate, making it one of the deepest compositions on Roots to Branches in several respects.

'Dangerous Veils' (Anderson)

The quicker woodwind opening fixes it to the previous tune, as does its narrative about Anderson watching a dancer to whom he dares not speak due to social mores ('I'm not inviting any fierce reaction / And I'm not one for naming holy names'). Once more, people are unable to socialise due to ideological barriers, and the chameleonic aggression slithers behind his sentiments with grandiose poise until Barre launches into a multidimensional solo while Bailey and Giddings boisterously stir around Perry's tight syncopation. More verses are followed by more go-getting theatrics, issuing another exquisite example of how exceptional the musicianship is throughout the record.

'Beside Myself' (Anderson)

While the arrangement of 'Beside Myself' is as extraordinarily lavish and changeable as anything else on the album – with gorgeous acoustic guitar, piano, strings, and bamboo flute keynotes pirouetting with penetrating heartache – it's Anderson's songwriting and singing that makes it the superlative selection on *Roots to Branches*. During his time in Bombay, he noticed the disparities between affluence and poverty (plus the things children needed to do to survive) and that distress floods his longings like they rarely have before. 'I'll wish you up a silver train / To carry you to school, bring you home again / Strip off that work paint / And put a cleaner face on / I'm beside myself'. The song is an unforgettable gem, plain and simple.

'Wounded, Old and Treacherous' (Anderson)

This song's lengthy picturesque-then-panicked jumping off point instils a heroic collocation to the monotone recollections of 'when love was the law' and 'a time for the tooth and claw' (both allusions to Tennyson's *In Memoriam*). This duality repeats without much deviation (except for the tremendous flute and guitar solos near the climax), so while its shifty but discerning rockiness and complexity is indisputably enthralling and pushy, it's a case of an amazing arrangement looping too much to justify the duration. (It wouldn't suffer if Anderson's vocals were removed, either, as they really don't add any melodic value.)

'At Last, Forever' (Anderson)

Much like Porcupine Tree's morose masterpiece 'Heartattack in a Layby', 'At Last, Forever' is about a man promising his wife that he'll stay with her even after he passes away. Its score is tastefully devastating, with piano and woodwind weeps, leading to resigned acoustic guitar strums, ardent orchestration, thoughtful drumming, and firm, graceful farewells ('But we'll cling together / Some kind of heaven written in your face'). In a sense, it's like a more reasoned, painful, and bombastic sequel to 'Wond'ring Aloud', too, in that it bittersweetly marks the end of a lifetime together that could've started with 'toast as the butter runs'. Either way, its stunning tragedy resonates boundlessly.

'Stuck in the August Rain' (Anderson)
It also seems tied to *Aqualung*'s domestic trinket in its warm security of returning home to a lover who 'brings Jasmine tea on a painted tray'. Sadly, the speaker is unable to fully appreciate the setting since he's still 'stuck in the August rain' (fixated on past hardships), and the instrumentation soars at capturing this inner tension in its segues between caring fortitude and irate comprehensions. Outside of Anderson and Barre's archetypical glories, the horns, low piano chords, and pondering outlines from Perry are crucial to ministering this oxymoronic notion of gratified melancholy.

'Another Harry's Bar' (Anderson)
Still channelling Mark Knopfler's cadence, Anderson seals this nostalgic piano ballad with unglamourised but sincere descriptions to drive home the stylish fragility of the adjoining timbres. Whereas so much of *Roots to Branches* is hostile and intricate, 'Another Harry's Bar' finishes the LP with polished ease until the fervent outro, resting on omniscient – but debatably autobiographical, as many fans quizzically believe that Harry represents a younger version of Anderson's talent and muse – composure to lull you into extensive contemplation. It's a stirring finale to a thoroughly fantastic sequence.

Bonuses
The remastered disc contains *no* extras at all, so fingers crossed that an expanded edition is put together in time for its twenty-fifth or thirtieth anniversary.

J-Tull Dot Com (1999)

Personnel:
Ian Anderson: vocals, acoustic guitar, flute, bouzouki, engineer, cover painting
Martin Barre: electric guitar, acoustic guitar, assistant engineer
Jonathan Noyce: bass guitar, assistant engineer
Doane Perry: drums, percussion, electric piano, assistant engineer
Andrew Giddings: keyboards, piano, Hammond organ, accordion, assistant engineer
Najma Akhtar: backing vocals (2)
Martyn Goddard: photography
Bogdan Zarkowski: design
Tim Matyear :assistant engineer
Produced at Ian Anderson's home studio, United Kingdom, Late 1998 – Early 1999 by Ian Anderson
UK and US release date: August 1999
Highest chart places: UK: 44, USA: 161
Running time: 54:20 (CD)
Current edition: EMI 2010 CD reissue

At last, we've reached the final Jethro Tull album of completely new material, released almost exactly thirty years after the first one (so that's a nice bow on one of the most quality, impactful, varied, and bold discographies in the history of rock music). Considering how artistically rich *Roots to Branches* was, it's no shock that they decided to stick to the same template for *J-Tull Dot Com*,albeit with a thinner World Music glaze and a thicker smattering of 'contemporary beats and production styles'. It's lyrics 'reflect on the new age of communication and the nature of ageing' – to embrace the new millennium). Frankly, aside from *A Passion Play*, it may be the most underrated studio item in their catalogue. In no way ground-breaking, it's far too heterogeneous and fetching to habitually be graded at the bottom of the pile, even if the title is too transparently eager to be trendy, and thus, instantly passé, although it did point fans to the website to hear early versions of tracks, among other things. Part of the reason, of course, is how successful Pegg's replacement, Jonathan Noyce, is at taking over (in fact, this line-up would remain until 2007, paradoxically instigating the longest unchanged roster in the group's lifespan). In any case, *J-Tull Dot Com* is much more enjoyable and commendable than the consensus dictates; it doesn't match *Roots to Branches*, but it's an unquestionably fitting swansong for Jethro Tull. Rarely does a band with such an unparalleled history go out on such a high note.

'Spiral' (Anderson)

Its peppy pick-up of woodwind swirls and electric guitar stabs induce the thematic awareness of waking from a dream and not quite knowing what's real and what's imagined. Although his voice is a bit strained – regrettably, a

115

defining trait of J-Tull Dot Com – Anderson still musters up very catchy stanzas (most notably during closing phrases such as 'Gathering momentum / On a Disneyesque adventure ride'). Likewise, Barre's chords tightly complement his every line while Noyce and Perry chart the path with proud resourcefulness. It's an exhilarating commencement that, deliberately or not, showcases why Jethro Tull still outshone the majority of younger rock bands.

'Dot Com' (Anderson)
'[A]n ode to the communication options of the Internet; two lovers in touch only via their corporate email accounts' – as Anderson explains on the promo CD – this commentary on the intersection of advanced technology and romance is a precursor to future genre explorations like Ayreon's 'Web of Lies' (performed by Phideaux Xavier and Epica's Simone Simons). Here, Anderson duets with the justly revered Indian singer Najma Akhtar, generating a beautifully airy blend of Asian textures that make up for its gently mawkish songwriting.

'AWOL' (Anderson)
Giddings and Anderson's hypnotic coil – coupled with belligerent assistance from the remaining trio – yields a stark divergence from Perry and Noyce's knocks in the verses. In fact, their keyboard and flute dramas continuously hoist the track (about an employee dreaming of ditching work to gallivant at casinos and eateries with 'the girl who's working nights') above the affable but ordinary track it would be otherwise. The sparse surrealism at the fadeaway, with its interlocking flourish of instruments, is a nice touch, too.

'Nothing @ All' (Giddings)
Giddings' minute-long piano soliloquy is a sorrowful listen, with imperative routes between distraught chords and otherworldly synths sparking judicious considerations and closure. His hammering of an E note across multiple octaves at the end is its most sobering moment, not to mention a powerful entrance into the demoralisation that comes next.

'Wicked Windows' (Anderson)
Just as *Roots to Branches* has the overwhelmingly effective 'Beside Myself', J-Tull Dot Com gifts us this, a heartrending 'reference to the heinous [Nazi] Heinrich Himmler'. After purchasing new reading glasses, Anderson dawned on how 'so many bad guys in history wore those little wire-rimmed spectacles; they lend an air of menace and cunning, disguised as the frailty of diminished eyesight'. Aptly, he wastes no time launching into mournful, downright Shakespearean echoes of the past, weeping pointed allusions like 'Now and then / Memories of men who loved me / No stolen kiss / Could match their march on hot coals for me' and 'Harsh truth for history to mellow / Through

my eyes / loyalties and obligation magnified' cutting to the core of the atrocity. The adjacent programmed percussion and tearful piano playing afford a nihilistic chill, and the flavourful and orchestral eruptions in-between the cracks are masterfully evocative. In every way, then, 'Wicked Windows' is one of Jethro Tull's greatest triumphs in over two decades.

'Hunt by Numbers' (Anderson)
Taking on a vastly smaller (pun intended) and less substantial topic that conjures Heavy Horses, 'Hunt by Numbers' is a joking jab at 'soft and silky nightwalkers' (better known as cats). Kicked off by a trademark union of flute, guitar, and keyboard riffs, it's a simple but effective and time-tested structure that grants treasurable levity after the weight of 'Wicked Windows'. Once again, the duo of Perry and Noyce plaster stanch rhythmic walls to house Barre, Anderson and Giddings' freak-outs, and Anderson sings with that malevolent glee he does so well. It's a fun chase, all things considered.

'Hot Mango Flush' (Barre, Anderson)
It's a hodgepodge of imagery related to the sights and sounds Barre and Anderson took in while on vacation in the Caribbean. Musically, there's an untroubled native buoyancy to its smooth guitar work, climbing woodwinds, and vibrant percussion; vocally, its spectator absurdism is most distinguished for giving us a glimpse into the spoken word panache of solo records like *Thick as a Brick 2* and *Homo Erraticus*. Taken as a sumptuous novelty more than anything else, it's a fun distraction.

'El Niño' (Anderson)
Obviously named after the destructive weather phases around the central and eastern tropical Pacific Ocean, 'El Niño' unleashes a downpour of heavy metal antipathy to disrupt the whimsical yet threatening serenity of Anderson's proclamations ('As one, wet merchants turn their eyes towards the west / Trade winds falter as if in dire consequence'). The combat between its wistful and wrathful arsenals is always gripping, even if its course would profit from a sliver more of multifarious sophistication.

'Black Mamba' (Anderson)
The juxtaposition between Giddings' imperial piano descents and the compound of Anderson, Barre, and Noyce's cyclical flees delivers a soothing false calm prior to the explosion of its symphonic rock groundwork. The temptation of the snake – an allegory for an ill-advised seduction by a woman brought on by 'dark thoughts of the sleepless' – authors an adequate parable, but it's the rowdy arrangement of 'Black Mamba' that's the best motive to dance with it.

'Mango Surprise' (Anderson)

Lasting only seventy seconds, it's basically a looser and more animated reimagining of the earlier entry without any words outside of Anderson chanting, 'Hot mango flush'. Instead, horns, animal noises, and miscellaneous cultural insignias are amalgamated for an entertainingly happy-go-lucky collage whose final place as a flashy intermezzo isn't totally worth the exertion.

'Bends Like a Willow' (Anderson)

There's a dry aura to Anderson's parched dedication to his 'fully armed angel' (wife) who's taken care of him after so many years of being 'swept in the riptide[s]' of existence. Oddly enough, it feels like a lost piece from an '80s LP due to its processed effects, yet it still works because of how much is going on the background at every moment. Perry is expressly dextrous around Barre and Anderson's ever-changing transitions, and Giddings synths add valuable if antiquated eccentricity.

'Far Alaska' (Anderson)

The urge to travel is conveyed efficiently in both its fancifully pressurised hustle-and-bustle movements and in its youthfully enthusiastic illustrations of 'Rio in the Carnival' while 'dream-arranging from the safety of [a] room'. It's another sturdy balance of mosaic flutters and potent bouts that is highlighted by its midsection frenzy of glued piano, flute, and electric guitar lines scattered around tricky rhythmic breaks, strings, and another model Barre solo. In fact, it recalls the virtuosic storm of 'Minstrel in the Gallery' – no small feat considering their age gap – in that peripheral trip.

'The Dog-Ear Years' (Anderson)

Every part encapsulates Anderson's celebratory gratefulness for a life well lived as a musician ('Rattling through airways / Plastic on cold trays') and husband ('You have settled beside me / To the far and the wide of me'). He quirkily sings while seizing *Thick as a Brick*-esque multi-layered warmth via acoustic guitar thrums, keen syncopation, and keyboard, woodwind, and horn embellishments. Halfway through, a prophetic and serious voice implores, 'For God's sake, keep moving', as if to say that he's not worn out yet. Judging by the eminence displayed here, he wasn't wrong.

'A Gift of Roses' (Anderson)

Alas, 'A Gift of Roses' is the nail in the coffin of Jethro Tull's brand new studio albums; luckily, however, it's a touching valediction not only for J-Tull Dot Com but to Jethro Tull's attainments en masse, as it emits earnest closure at each festive hard rock turn. His opening invitation – 'I count the hours; you count the days / Together, we count the minutes in this Passion Play' – is a lovely meta-reference geared toward the loved ones who've been there all long (fans alongside friends and family). There's a jubilant acceptance in his carriages, and Giddings' accordion aids the token instruments in bringing the bittersweet party to recognition. It's the perfect ending credits for Jethro Tull's journey, leaving all involved to move on together in appreciation of what they brought to popular music over the past thirty years.

I'd be remiss not to mention that on some versions of the CD, a period of silence separates 'A Gift of Roses' from the secret title track of Anderson's then-upcoming solo album, *The Secret Language of Birds*. A short introduction plays in advance of it. Since it's not an official part of *J-Tull Dot Com*, however, we won't delve any more into it now.

Bonuses
As with *Roots to Branches*, no version of *J-Tull Dot Com* comes with any bonuses, which is a shame since it definitely deserves some.

The Jethro Tull Christmas Album (2003)

Personnel:
Ian Anderson: vocals, acoustic guitar, flute, mandolin, percussion, piccolo
Martin Barre: electric guitar, acoustic guitar
Jonathan Noyce: bass guitar
Doane Perry: drums, percussion
Andrew Giddings: keyboards, accordion
James Duncan: additional drums and percussion
Dave Pegg: additional bass guitar and mandolin
The Sturcz String Quartet: violins, viola, cello
Alex Ivanovich: engineer
Kenny Wheeler: engineer
Nick Watson: mastering
Igor Vereshagin: photography
Produced at The Town House, London, Early – Mid 2003 by Ian Anderson
UK and US release date: September 2003
Highest chart places: UK: none, USA: none
Running time: 62:16 (CD)
Current edition: EMI 2009 CD reissue with *Live – Christmas At St Bride's 2008* bonus CD

For someone who'd been so openly critical and cynical regarding Christianity – well, organised religion overall – in the past, it's surprising that Anderson agreed when the record company (specifically, Fuel 2000 boss Len Fico) suggested Jethro Tull release an album for the holiday. Indeed, he'd originally declined for fear of it being 'altogether cheesy and trivial', but eventually he found a way to stack applicable material already in the repertoire with 'some variations on Christmas carols, looking at the "other side" of Christmas'. Combined, they produce a steadily invigorating and endearing yuletide yarn that, as Dave Sleger wrote in his review for AllMusic, 'folds so easily into the rest of their output' because it 'recapture[s] the musical intensity of three decades' past' while also meeting the expectations of a commercial seasonal collection.

In the booklet to the CD, Anderson clarifies his views on Christmas as follows:

I'm not exactly a practising paid-up Christian but I have grown up and lived with a so-called Christian society for 55 years and still feel great warmth for the nostalgia, festive occasion and family togetherness, so much a part of that time of year. Maybe without Christmas we would have that much less to celebrate and enjoy in this troubled old world. But it's really all the Winter Solstice and the re-birth of nature overlaid with the common sense and righteous teachings of Mr. C.

A Christmas in this modern world should, in my view, accommodate the leisure needs and affections of Muslims, Hindus, Buddhists, atheists and agnostics, as well as Fido the family dog and Felix the cat. Throw in a few lost cousins and that dreadful man from next door and you have it! Sip the sloe gin, pull a cracker (so long as she's not the daughter of that dreadful man from next door), kiss and cuddle under the mistletoe, toss Vegan disciplines aside, gobble the turkey (steady on, now) and have a therapeutic respite from the rigours of daily life.

Christmas – an aspirin for the soul or cold-turkey celebration of the birth and life of Christ? It has to be a measured bit of both, doesn't it?

Logically, the *J-Tull Dot Com* crew returns, as do Pegg and Anderson's son, James Duncan; this lineage (by both profession and blood) gives it a suitable familial magic. Also on staff is the Sturcz String Quartet – leader/cellist András Sturcz, violist Gyula Benk , 2nd violinist Péter Szilágyi, and 1st violinist Gábor Csonka – whose abundance of classical fervour is a priceless part of the festivities. Since Anderson was also working on his fourth solo outing, Rupi's Dance (which came out a month before *The Jethro Tull Christmas Album* and leads into it by having its last track, 'Birthday Card at Christmas', return as the starting one here), they had to do more remote recording and mixing than usual.

While no UK and US chart placements can be found, the band attests that The Jethro Tull Christmas Album was 'an unexpected critical and commercial success'. Debatably, it can't be measured against its predecessors since it's not a wholly new project, yet it's still looked upon fondly overall by patrons and the press. Joining Sleger in admiration, for instance, are *Sea of Tranquility*'s Steve Fleck, *Vintage Rock*'s Shawn Perry, and *Rolling Stone*'s Sandy Masuo (who concludes, 'Few things are more festive than accomplished musicians having a dickens of a good time, and that's what this album is all about'). It's hard to argue against that.

'Birthday Card at Christmas' (Anderson)
Dedicated to his daughter, Gael, who, 'like millions of other unfortunates, celebrates her birthday within a gnat's whisker of Christmas', the flute hook with acoustic guitar accompaniment is a guaranteed earworm. Anderson sings with the honoured initiative and patriarchal pride, too, and presents one of his best solos in years in the middle of the gaiety (held to task by Perry's commanding syncopation). It's a joyous commitment all-around.

'Holly Herald' (trad. arranged by Anderson, 'Herald' by Wesley and Mendelssohn)
It's a melding of the traditional British carol 'The Holly and The Ivy' and Wesley and Mendelssohn's 'Hark! The Herald Angels Sing'. Thunderous drumming gives way to accordion and woodwind dominance as other instrumental stockings – acoustic guitar, chimes, keyboard – hang with merriment around them. There are also a couple of edgy bridges during the second half that are a

121

nice change of pace and make the chief rendition even more densely cheerful. In total, it's an attractive testament to Jethro Tull's ability to execute others' works with characteristic excellence.

'Christmas Song' (Anderson)
Originally released as a UK single in 1968 – and then included on 1972's *Living in the Past* compilation – this version is very similar to the original if a tad slower and more welcoming. The initial sleigh bells at the start are more pronounced and adorned with more timbres, and the strings from the original are gone (to name a couple of differences). Vocally, Anderson's rebuke of selfishness and indulgence sound remarkably close to how he did as a young man. As a whole, this take isn't a drastic rebirth, though.

'Another Christmas Song' (Anderson)
Similarly, the far more recent 'Another Christmas Song' has few adjustments from its *Rock Island* counterpart. Really, you'd need a spectrograph to discern much at all aside from its ever so slightly kinder yet fuller ornamentation. It is nice to know that Pegg returned to duplicate his contribution to it.

'God Rest Ye Merry Gentlemen' (trad. arranged by Anderson)
Tull first tackled this centuries-old standard as part of a medley on 1978's live double album, *Bursting Out*, and it's pretty much a compulsory inclusion on *The Jethro Tull Christmas Album*. That's not to say it's unsought or poor, of course; on the contrary, its unremitting melodic mellowness as Anderson, Barre, and Giddings take turns in the limelight is inarguably delightful and faithful, catching an easy-going vibe that harkens back to the band's late 1960s primers. Their urbane gothic team-up near the end is exclusively beguiling.

'Jack Frost and the Hooded Crow' (Anderson)
It's an outtake from *The Broadsword and the Beast* that later saw the light of day as the B-side to 1986's 'Coronach' UK single (as well as part of the *20 Years of Jethro Tull* boxset). It's as pastoral and intricate as the aforementioned bonus track on the *Broadsword and the Beast* remaster, but with more grounded production (most notably, the percussion) and less agitation in Anderson's inflexions. As such, it's the superior version, with some of the most infectious harmonies and altruistically motivating key changes of their entire history.

'Last Man at the Party' (Anderson)
Only Anderson, Giddings, and Barre appear on this quasi Celtic rhyming chant about colourful friends and neighbours who 'come around' to 'raise a glass to good comradery'. Texturally, its use of piccolo and mandolin makes it one of the most epic and multifaceted pieces on record, as it relentlessly modulates

around its commemorative verses like the precursor to Trans-Siberian Orchestra. The emphasis on accordion and flute voyages in the middle really drives home the holiday spirit, too.

'Weathercock' (Anderson)

Like previous revisions, this one doesn't stray very far from the *Heavy Horses* original, but it does feel a pinch more controlled, calm, and clear in general (as intangible as that may sound). For example, Barre's electric guitar work is sharper and more protruding than on the hazier 1978 interpretation, whereas more even attention is granted to all the decorations this time around. It's certainly not an apples and oranges comparison, however.

'Pavane' (Anderson, original arrangement by Gabriel Fauré)

Gabriel Fauré's late nineteenth-century score receives a lavishly folkish treatment from the quintet of Anderson, Barre, Giddings, Noyce, and Duncan (who's just as adept as Perry at spicing up and cooling down his role depending on what's needed). The acoustic guitar lines and orchestration rival the woodwinds and piano as the most mesmerising feature, and it effortlessly reminds one of the influence Jethro Tull had on many current progressive metal artists from Sweden, Finland, and Norway.

'First Snow on Brooklyn' (Anderson)

'First Snow on Brooklyn' is the only selection with the Sturcz String Quartet. Naturally, they do a highly modest yet marvellous job providing a charming foundation for the main ensemble's tender swaths and surveys of how special it is to return to New York's 'Christmas card upon the pavement'. As with many of Anderson's tales of polarised homecomings, there's also a touch of trepidation and redemption as he asks himself, 'Is it such a good idea that I am here again?' Amidst 'rocky memories', 'choking tears', 'deep regrets' and 'heavy heartbeats'; this cognitive dissonance allows for more depth as it pinpoints the healing power of atonement and connection at Christmas time. Even absolutely secular listeners will be moved by it.

'Greensleeved' (Anderson, based on trad. 'Greensleeves')

The reverberating woodwind motif is unavoidably arresting, the underlying keyboard chord changes are prettily emotive, and the acoustic guitar swipes and arpeggios are studied and elegant. The clean guitar and piano solos are alluring, too, and Noyce impresses as the systematic backbone. All in all, it's about what you'd expect from a Jethro Tull reading of the Elizabethan classic.

'Fire at Midnight' (Anderson)

It's a modernised rebranding of the *Songs from the Wood* closer, and despite being 95% the same, it's the little alterations that make the former form best this one. There's less fairy-tale peculiarity to it (the recurrent Cathedral croons are absent, as are some other pagan accessories), and Anderson's phrasing and pitch are marginally off, which, while understandable, nonetheless takes away from its charisma. Put another way, just about all of the parts are there but they're assembled more mechanically, losing much of the enchanted sensation in the development.

'We Five Kings' (Anderson, based on 'We Three Kings' by Rev. J. Hopkins)

A wordless attempt at Hopkins' 1857 carol, it's relatively inventive, with Duncan and Noyce's hip opening theme lingering as the track's most representative element. In addition, Giddings' piano and accordion supplements very much stand out around Barre and Anderson's foremost charges. Honestly, 'We Five Kings' is perhaps the most extreme and idiosyncratic adoption on *The Jethro Tull Christmas Album* (which makes sense since many other radical deviations are out there, so there aren't as many essentials to uphold anyway).

'Ring Out Solstice Bells' (Anderson)

Another Songs from the Wood tune-up, it – like 'Fire at Midnight' – is more of a tune-down since its less compressed and hospitable (and more robotically refined). It is more accurate than the other one, though, with a higher percentage of nuances upheld and a stronger approximation of the vocals (including the harmonies). By and large, it's a matching clone.

'Bourée' (J.S. Bach, arrangement by Anderson)

In contrast to the erstwhile updates, 'Bourée' is significantly transformed from its Stand Up base. For one thing, it's more urgent and busy from the jump, with a higher octave for the flute and the bass line counterpoint being replaced by guitar intervals. Afterwards, more players mean more instrumentation and variety, with accordion and harpsichord complementing new and old passages. However, the 1969 edition felt rawer and more striving – whereas this is more dignified and unworried – so neither definitively beats the other.

'A Winter Snowscape' (Barre)

Barre's introductory acoustic arpeggios are hypnotically irregular, and his encrusted counterpoints – as well as Anderson's – magnify the stylish yuletide splendour. Its prolonged diversions are just as sentimentally cultured and the gradual build-up of metronomic percussive pings and piano during the second half is immensely faint yet vital to its endurance. Above all else, it's the latest in a long line of reasons for why Barre could always hold his own against his peers but rarely earned the same amount of esteem.

Bonuses

Live – Christmas At St Bride's 2008 is a must-own add-on. Beyond offering some stuff from *The Jethro Tull Christmas Album*, it contains a handful of new choir performances ('Silent Night', 'Oh, Come All Ye Faithful', and 'Gaudete') and Jethro Tull favourites (namely, 'Jack in the Green' and an excerpt of *Thick as a Brick*). It's the final official recording of Jethro Tull, too, and that alone makes it indispensable.

Roundup – Live/Video, Compilations, and EPs/B-Sides

Live/Video

We haven't really discussed live Jethro Tull much thus far, so let's dig into the major releases now (in order of recording, not release). The first, *Nothing is Easy: Live at the Isle of Wight 1970*, was taped on the fifth and last day of the festival (August 31ˢᵗ), when the band played in-between The Moody Blues and Jimi Hendrix as the second act on the bill. It finds the *Benefit* line-up – Anderson, Cornick, Evan, Barre, and Bunker – in top form as they reproduce classic early tracks like 'With You There to Help Me', 'We Used to Know / For a Thousand Mothers', a lengthier vocal version of 'Dharma for One', and even a bit of foreshadowing to 1971's *Aqualung* via 'My God'. A few added guitar, piano, flute, and drum solos help the set flow as well, and an accompanying DVD offers a fascinating visual complement with a few alterations ('To Cry You a Song' and 'With You There to Help Me' aren't included; however, there are longer renditions of 'Dharma for One' and 'My God').

Live at Carnegie Hall 1970 sees them playing a similar set on November 4 in New York City as part of an anti-drug drive; it was later put out on a special edition of Stand Up, and an abridged vinyl version came to light as part of Record Store Day on April 18, 2015. In 1978, arguably their most popular live album, Bursting Out, became the first one officially issued. Recorded at various places during the European *Heavy Horses* tour in May and June (including the Bern Festhalle in Switzerland), the full set was unleashed in 2004 and contains some of the band's best material ever, including 'Jack in the Green', 'Songs from the Wood', 'Minstrel in the Gallery' and 'Sweet Dream'. It also contains introductions by Anderson and Montreux Jazz Festival founder Claude Nobs and the 'Conundrum' and 'Dambusters March' instrumentals. Its most noteworthy inclusion, however, is the shortened 'Thick as a Brick', which, while inherently blasphemous (such a masterpiece shouldn't be cut down at all if you ask me), does a good enough job of spotlighting its greatest moments. In support of *Busting Out*, they also played a comparable set at Madison Square Garden in October 1978, marking the first time a rock group appeared live from America on British television (specifically, the *Old Grey Whistle Test*, whose footage also arrived on DVD with the 2009 package). Tragically, it's also noteworthy for having an old friend, Tony Williams, take over bass duties since Glascock was – to put it bluntly – near death.

1980's A tour spawned the already explored Slipstream, and a few years later, *Live at Hammersmith '84* captured Anderson, Barre, Perry, Vettese, and Pegg at the Odeon on September 9 (in support of *Under Wraps*). Sadly, its strongest attribute is its juxtaposition of the weaker current material ('Under Wraps #1' and 'Pussy Willow') with the stronger earlier stuff ('Living in the Past' and 'Hunting Girl'). Still, it's a solid document of the period, as is 1988's 20 Years of Jethro Tull feature that contains interviews with members, fans, and related insiders in-between clips of live sets and music videos ('Heavy Horses', 'Steel Monkey', and 'The Whistler', to name a few).

A Little Light Music is notable for basically being Jethro Tull Unplugged since it was recorded during a May 1992 semi-acoustic run in Europe and the Middle East. Greek vocalist George Dalaras sings 'John Barleycorn' with Anderson and other selections, such as 'One White Duck', 'Life Is a Long Song', and 'From a Dead Beat to an Old Greaser', are especially moving in this form. As for the players, Perry and newcomer Giddings were absent; in their place, Fairport Convention's Dave Mattacks fulfilled their roles, leading many to deem the quartet Fairport Tull and Jethro Convention. As you'd expect, Jack in the Green: Live in Germany 1970–1993 – which came out in 2008 – encapsulates various performances in the country over that time and offers some real gems ('Thick as a Brick' and 'Improvisation II').

The Millennium collection begins with the *Living with the Past* CD/DVD, a blend of content from the November 2001 Hammersmith Apollo show, miscellaneous songs from the group's history, and even a couple of pieces from Anderson's solo work ('The Habanero Reel' and 'In the Grip of Stronger Stuff'). It's a fairly comprehensive overview of their career, with multiple line-ups represented. 2003's A *New Day Yesterday* (aka *Jethro Tull: A New Day Yesterday – 25th Anniversary Collection, 1969-1994*) is a DVD comprising live appearances from around the world, promos, rehearsal footage, and TV clips. Standouts include 'The Story of the Hare Who Lost His Spectacles', 'Aqualung' live at BBC Sight & Sound 1977, '25th Anniversary Rehearsals / My God', and 'Teacher' live on French TV 1970). The same year, *Live at Montreux* offered the sights and sounds of Jethro Tull's career-spanning set at the Montreux Jazz Festival (with 'Empty Café', 'Eurology' and 'New Jig' appealing as three rare instrumentals). Recorded in front of an audience at XM Studios in Washington, DC, 2005's *Aqualung Live* was an unsuccessful but worthwhile attempt by Anderson, Barre, Giddings, Noyce, and Perry to improve upon the original. It includes the whole album and excerpts of the band speaking to the crowd. It was given away at US concerts in October and November 2005; as for Europe, royalties fittingly went to various charities for the homeless. Lastly, *Around the World Live* arrived in 2013 and is a four-DVD set of concert footage from 1970 to 2005. Obviously, just about every member of Jethro Tull is included somewhere, and there's tons of variety between the multitude of venues (including the 1970 Isle of Wight Festival, Tampa, FL, Munich, Dortmund, Holland, and Switzerland).

Compilations
To avoid verbosity and repetition, I'll similarly only focus on the primary list of these assemblages as well. It starts with Jethro Tull's most well-known, 1972's *Living in the Past*. Peaking at #3 in the US (and going gold shortly thereafter) and at #13 in the UK, its assortment of studio tracks, outtakes, and the like

is distinguished for including the full Life is a Long Song EP and the majority of the non-LP singles. It includes the original UK version of 'Teacher' that was the B-side of 'The Witch's Promise', many of which were converted from mono to stereo. Like Benefit, the UK and US versions differed slightly, with the latter replacing 'Inside' and 'Locomotive Breath' with 'Hymn 43' and 'Alive and Well and Living In', respectively. While initial CD editions also varied in their sequences (chiefly due to time constraints), the modern edition includes everything. As for the cover of Living in the Past – among Jethro Tull's most emblematic, for sure – and packaging, its gate-fold housed a sizeable colour booklet of over fifty photos. It's truly a must-have gathering. Four years later, *M.U. – The Best of Jethro Tull* appeared (with its continuation, *Repeat – The Best of Jethro Tull – Vol II*, coming in 1977). Together, they span 1969 – 1976 and their most enticing contributions are the previously unreleased (at least in the UK and US) 'Rainbow Blues' (a feisty symphonic romp) and 'Glory Row' (an eccentric rocker highlighted by honouring horns). The first of the pair was also re-released as The Essential in 2003.

Halfway into the 1980s, Original Masters repeats some of the material from the two Best of LPs while also adding 'Sweet Dream', 'Songs from the Wood', 'The Witch's Promise', and 'Life is a Long Song' (so it strangely doesn't include anything after 1977). Thankfully, 1988's *20 Years of Jethro Tull* (not to be confused with the aforementioned video) does a superb job at representing rarities, radio selections, and what they deem 'flawed gems' (such as 'Rhythm in God', 'Overhang', 'The Chateau D'Isaster Tapes: Scenario/Audition/No Rehearsal', and 'Motoreyes') across its expansive vinyl, cassette, and CD releases (all of which were boxed in 12x12 inch cardboard with a 24-page booklet).

1993 birthed three important entries. First, the 25th Anniversary Box Set, a limited-edition amalgamation of content (some previously unavailable) from 1969 – 1992 whose four discs were broken up as follows: 'Remixed', 'Carnegie Hall, N.Y.', 'The Beacons Bottom' (new takes on mostly older standards), and 'Pot Pourri' (international live material). Later, the invaluable Nightcap finally let fans hear the full remnants of the 'Chateau D'Isaster Tapes', as well as unreleased stuff from between 1974 and 1991 (like extras from the *War Child* and *Broadsword and the Beast* sessions). Once again, proceeds from it went to charity. Finally, *The Best of Jethro Tull – The Anniversary Collection* is an in-depth retrospective of album tracks from 1968 to 1991 (without any real frills).

Anderson handpicked the twenty pieces on 2001's *The Very Best Of* and edited songs like 'Heavy Horses', 'Too Old to Rock 'n' Roll: Too Young to Die!', and 'Minstrel in the Gallery' for time. (The lack of anything from *J-Tull Dot Com* seems an oversight.) 2007's self-explanatory *The Best of Acoustic* is a thorough recap of many Jethro Tull jewels and some solo Ian Anderson tunes ('Rupi's Dance' and 'The Water Carrier'). Likely the most definitive of them all, *50 for 50* is a treasurable overview that truly covers the earliest to latest eras, with 'Critique Oblique', 'This Whistler', 'A Song for Jeffrey', 'Fylingdale Flyer' and

'Budapest' among its irreplaceable index.

EPs/B-Sides
Life Is A Long Song EP (1971)

Jethro Tull's pinnacle EP, the five-track *Life is a Long Song* was put out on September 3, 1971 and charted at #11 in the UK. A delightfully sobering and quick acoustic ballad with increasingly prevalent classical and piano coatings, the opening title track is not only the best of the bunch but also one of Anderson's truly timeless lone outings. Next, 'Up the Pool' places a bluesy bass beneath tight acoustic guitar chords and Anderson's reserved multilayered glee. Interestingly, the percussion picks up as it goes, and some background banter makes it feel like a lived-in aural space. The third inclusion, 'Dr. Bogenbroom', nails the yowling darkness of *Benefit* with its shifts between mellow and ominous instrumentation (all of which breathe life into Anderson's exasperated tell-offs), whereas 'For Later' is a ruthlessly complex jam that perfectly mixes their bluesy roots with the progressive rock eccentricities of *Aqualung* and its follow-up epics. Closer 'Nursie', on the other hand, is the shortest and simplest of them all, offering another instance of Anderson's solo acoustic elegance in the guise of 'Wond'ring Aloud' or the still-to-come "One White Duck / 010 = Nothing at All'. Considering its sizeable variety and consistent quality, it's no wonder why *Life is a Long Song* is such an adored release.

The fact that Jethro Tull crafted only a few EPs is surprising. The earliest, *Best 4*, came out in Japan and includes 'Bourée', 'Living in the Past', 'Sweet Dream', and 'Love Story'. Next, *Life is a Long Song* was put out on September 3, 1971 and completed its five-song duration with 'Up the Pool', 'Dr. Bogenbroom', 'For Later', and Nursie'. In 1972, *This is Jethro Tull* brought 'Living in the Past', 'Locomotive Breath', 'Hymn 43', and 'Song for Jeffrey' to Australia, while four years on, *Christmas* packs in 'Ring Out Solstice Bells', 'March, the Mad Scientist', 'Christmas Song', and 'Pan Dance' (a classical instrumental). Jethro Tull ended the decade with 1979's *Home*, which also gifted 'King Henry's Madrigal', 'Warm Sporran', and 'Solstice Bells'. Ten years hence, Bolivia's *Crest of a Knave* trio (one of the group's rarest records) consisted of 'Steel Monkey', 'Jump Start', and 'Budapest'. Peru's 1992 venture *Rocks on the Road* was more of an eight-song career overview than anything else; and 2004's second Christmas EP (sometimes called *Ring Out Solstice Bells* or *Merry Christmas from Jethro Tull*) showcases 'Ring Out Solstice Bells' and two live recordings: 'God Rest Ye Merry Gentlemen' and 'Slipstream'.

As for singles and B-sides, there are a handful of additional ones not yet chronologically observed that warrant attention (in other words, ones that contained non-album tracks). For instance, 1968's 'Sunshine Day / Aeroplane' is infamous for incorrectly listing the band as Jethro Toe (correctly spelt ones are counterfeits). Both of them would've fit fine on *This Was*, as would 'One for John Gee' (the B-side of 'A Song for Jeffrey'). The next year, 'Driving Song' and '17' complemented the 'Living in the Past' and 'Sweet Dream' A-sides, respectively. Interestingly, several "Edit" cuts of *A Passion Play* arrived in 1973, while the 'Minstrel in the Gallery' single was fleshed out by 'Summerday Sands'. In 1976, 'Rainbow Blues' first emerged as the UK B-side to 'Too Old to Rock 'n' Roll: Too Young to Die!', while 1977 brought the jolly 'Strip Cartoon' alongside lead option 'The Whistler' and 1978 coupled the choral rowdiness of 'A Stitch in Time' with 'Sweet Dream'.

1984's 'Lap of Luxury' also soared with electronic ode 'Astronomy', whereas 'Down at the End of Your Road' (a blasé ballad) paired with 1987's 'Steel Monkey'. The following year, 'Part of the Machine' was turned into a CD maxi-single with a few other picks – including the moody 'Stormy Monday Blues' – while 1991's 'This is Not Love' was joined by the nasally 'Night in the Wilderness'. Last but not least, 1992's expansive 'Rocks on the Road' supplied the 'Jack-A-Lynn' acoustic lament home demo; 1993's 'Living in the (Slightly More Recent) Past' came with 'Silver River Turning', 'Rosa on the Factory Floor', and 'I Don't Want to Be Me' (none of which are very good), and 1999's 'Bends Like a Willow' hands over the stiff 'It All Trickles Down' at no added cost.

End Game – Ian Anderson Solo
The bulk of this section will deal with Anderson's last two solo albums (*Thick as a Brick 2* and *Homo Erraticus*) since they're directly related to Jethro Tull concepts, but each of his LPs deserves some examination.

Walk into Light (1983)
Predating Under Wraps by a year, this arranging and songwriting partnership with Vettese is very much the marginally older sibling to it (for better or worse). Although that same shallowness does prove detrimental to some selections – 'Trains' and 'Different Germany', mostly – there are many good moments scattered about. For instance, the singing and instrumentation on opener 'Fly by Night' is emotional, tasteful, and catchy, while 'End Game' has enjoyable harmonies, 'Toad in the Hole' entices with its twisty musicianship, and 'Looking for Eden' manages heroic fantasy within its programmed shell. Honestly, it's more economical and bearable than the Jethro Tull counterpart as a whole.

Divinities: Twelve Dances with God (1995)
It's an entirely instrumental album that's influenced by religious themes and various ethnic musical backgrounds (such as African, Spanish, and Celtic). This time, Giddings and Perry were the Jethro Tull brethren brought on board (alongside many classical instrumentalists and timbres, including bamboo flute). According to Anderson, he wasn't initially excited about what the label (EMI) wanted but then became eager to take up 'the challenge of writing a large body of instrumental work'. So, how did it turn out? Pretty well, actually, with an eclectically worldly persona and a gracefully seamless movement. The blissful flutes and natural ambience of starter "In a Stone Circle" make it one of the most peaceful pieces. Subsequently, 'In the Grip of Stronger Stuff' is both playful and panicked (with engaging horns, strings, and organic percussion), 'At the Father's Knee' mixes suspenseful wonder and thunderous foreshadowing, and 'In the Pay of Spain' is a serene display of counterpoints and intrigue. Granted, you have to be of certain tastes to enjoy this kind of music in general, but those who do will love getting lost in what Anderson does with it.

The Secret Language of Birds (2000)
'Named after the dawn chorus, the natural sound of birds heard at dawn, most noticeably in the spring', Anderson's third solo release is a pseudo new Jethro Tull project since it also features Giddings, Conway, Barre, and James Duncan (plus drummer Darrin Mooney). Each song is coupled with an introduction, and as discussed earlier, the title track connects the start of *The Secret Language of Birds* to the end of *J-Tull Dot Com*. Stylistically, it's certainly the most traditional and fulfilling one yet, with the same flavour as the

group's final few ventures, more or less. Apexes include the dramatic yet restful acoustic number 'The Little Flower Girl', the symphonic Middle East essence of 'A Better Moon', the carefree stroll of "Sanctuary", and the wide-ranging European tension of closer 'The Stormont Shuffle'.

Rupi's Dance (2003)

According to Rabey, *Rupi's Dance* was meant to fulfil the request of 'fans and record companies alike ... [for] an acoustic album representing the type of material such as "Look into the Sun" from *Stand Up*'. While it doesn't quite satisfy that specific leaning, it nevertheless proffers plenty of fanciful, spacious, and regal inclusions to draw comparisons to the 'folk rock trilogy' (due in part to the aid of the Sturcz String Quartet, James Duncan, Barre, Perry, and Giddings, as well as keyboardist – and current Jethro Tull member – John O'Hara). 'Calliandra Shade (The Cappuccino Song)' introduces the LP with recreational discernment before 'Lost in Crowds' adds electric defiance, 'Old Black Cat' broods with acoustic and woodwind contemplation, and 'Two Short Planks' evokes the jubilance of 'Skating Away on the Thin Ice of the New Day'. Of course, the finale, 'Birthday Card at Christmas', leads into The Jethro Tull Christmas Album (further validating the argument that at least some of Anderson's catalogue is also canon in the Jethro Tull repository).

Thick as a Brick 2: Whatever Happened to Gerald Bostock? (2012)

Sequels rarely live up to, let alone surpass, the originals (especially if that first one is so celebrated and the follow-up comes decades after it). Such is the case with *Thick as a Brick 2* (henceforth referred to as TAAB 2 for brevity), a successor forty years in the making that – let's be honest – just about every fan dreaded and deemed downright sacrilegious. It's flat-out miraculous, then, that the record ended up being so great. By no means on par with the 1972 masterpiece, it's exponentially more competent and captivating than it has any right to be, demonstrating how much conceptual and technical brilliance Anderson retained after all those years.

It was mixed by Steven Wilson and also featured O'Hara (accordion, piano, keyboards, Hammond organ), Florian Opahle (electric guitar), Scott Hammond (percussion, drums), David Goodier (bass, glockenspiel), Peter Judge (trumpet, flugelhorn, tenor horn, E-flat tuba), and Ryan O'Donnell (additional vocals). To update the packaging, the physical periodical gimmick became the St. Cleve online newspaper, and it charted relatively well in the US and UK (#55 and #35, respectively). As for the official synopsis of the narrative, it's as follows:

[TAAB 2] presents five divergent, hypothetical life stories for Gerald Bostock, including a greedy investment banker, a homosexual homeless man, a soldier in the Afghan War, a sanctimonious evangelist preacher, and a most ordinary man who (married and childless) runs a corner store; by the end of the album, however, all five possibilities seem to converge in a similar concluding moment of gloomy or pitiful solitude.

While the numerous references to *Thick as a Brick* are blatant fan service, they don't feel nearly as obligatory and rough as they could. Rather, they blend with the new material quite well to truly make the sequence – a continuous statement broken into thirteen segments instead of two – feel unified and tied to its forebear. (In fact, it begins like the third half of the original and ends the same way, too, which can't help but make you smile.) For the most part, the new content is modern yet laudably vintage (so it wouldn't have been out of place as part of Jethro Tull's early 1970s arsenal). The multiple "Pebble" motifs are undoubtedly peaks, as are the thrilling pathos of 'Banker Bets, Banker Wins', the multifaceted thrusts of 'Adrift and Dumbfounded', the sorrowful sandiness of 'Wootton Bassett Town', and the experienced hypnosis of 'A Change of Horses'. Anderson's multiple spoken word passages are a bit odd initially, but they soon feel at home, too, and add some tongue-in-cheek novelty. In the end, TAAB 2 was never going to equal its precursor, yet you'd be hard pressed to find many follow-ups in any format that come as close.

Homo Erraticus (2014)

A mere two years later, Anderson returned with the same crew (sans Peter Judge) to continue the *Thick as a Brick* series. (Also, Steven Wilson was replaced by Jakko Jakszyk, and Carl Glover helmed the artwork and photography.) To be clearer, *Homo Erraticus* sees Bostock as a 'wondering man' in his fifties who 'recently discovered in his town's bookstore a "dusty, unpublished manuscript [*Homo Erraticus* (The St. Cleve Chronicles)], written by local amateur historian Ernest T. Parritt, (1873 -1928)"'. Thus, the lyrics are 'Bostock's resulting interpretation of Parritt's "illustrated document which summarises key historical elements of early civilisation in Britain and seems to prophesy future scenarios too"'. It's convoluted and meta, yes – in the liner notes, Anderson discusses the project as if Bostock were his neighbour prior to giving Bostock (as 'the lyricist') his own foreword – but that doesn't prevent it from being a damn fine extension of the lore (and of Anderson's madcap genius).

Nostalgia aside, *Homo Erraticus* may even top TAAB 2 as it infuses more 'medieval ... [and] heavy metal' traces in the midst of branching out from TAAB 2's overarching formula (including monologues) and knack for recurrent themes. 'Part One: Chronicles' presents the gritty but majestic and theatrical 'Doggerland' to set the stage; later, 'Enter the Uninvited' is ferociously mystical around Anderson's pop culture references, 'Meliora Sequamur' is daintily operatic (thanks to O'Donnell's thespian timbre), and 'The Pax Britannica' is a barstool piano sing-along with great performances from all involved.

The remaining two sections – 'Prophecies' and 'Revelations', respectively – make the second half of *Homo Erraticus* just as outstanding. For instance, the jazzy repetition and key changes of the wordless 'Tripudium Ad Bellum' install a fashionably complex vibe, whereas 'New Blood, Old Veins' is rhythmically entrancing and youthfully dynamic. The synthy jam 'The Browning of the Green' plays with the main theme of the record in resourceful ways and closer 'Cold Dead Reckoning' affords cataclysmic closure that leaves a few final moments of moving starriness in its wake. Altogether, *Homo Erraticus* is a superb journey that suggests even greater possibilities if and when Anderson goes on another fresh adventure. At the risk of infuriating readers, I dare say that *TAAB 2* and *Homo Erraticus* are better than anything Jethro Tull did after *Stormwatch*, as good as some of those latter recordings are.

Jethro Tull – The String Quartets (2017)

Considering that the only other Tull member here (O'Hara) wasn't a member until the latter half of the 2000s, it seems best to discuss *Jethro Tull – The String Quartets* here rather than as part of its namesake's discography. With assistance from the Carducci Quartet (violist Eoin Schmidt Martin, cellist Emma Denton, and violinists Michelle Fleming and Matthew Denton), Anderson and O'Hara set out to reimagine many of the band's superlative creations, albeit with 'rather cryptic [alternate] names' in order to avoid the complications of 'publishing and recording royalty payments' that arise 'when the same song title applies to different albums, performers and writers', as Anderson confesses. As for the renditions themselves, each one efficaciously tailors their origin to the new setting (even combining it with another Jethro Tull classic – 'Songs and Horses' – or an outside composition – 'We Used to Bach'). Aside from those, 'Only the Giving' finds Anderson recapturing the magnificence of 'Wond'ring Aloud, 'Velvet Gold' is predictable but filling, and 'Aquafugue' is unexpectedly tangential yet authentic, too.

Jordan Blum's ultimate Jethro Tull Playlist

There are some obvious choices here for sure, and some not so obvious ones, too. While there are certainly many great songs missing — and some that I'd rank higher than ones on this list —this set is my best attempt at compromising quality and range in terms of all the music that Jethro Tull offered from start to finish.

1. 'A Passion Play' (Complete)
2. 'Thick as a Brick' (Complete)
3. 'Aqualung'
4. 'Songs from the Wood'
5. 'Baker Street Muse'
6. 'Minstrel in the Gallery'
7. 'Cup of Wonder'
8. 'One White Duck | $0 \wedge \{10\}$ = Nothing At All'
9. 'Son'
10. 'The Whistler'
11. 'Fire at Midnight'
12. 'With You There to Help Me'
13. 'Weathercock'
14. 'Elegy'
15. 'Wond'ring Aloud'
16. 'Protect and Survive'
17. 'Beside Myself'
18. 'For Michael Collins, Jeffrey and Me'
19. 'Wicked Windows'
20. 'Living in the Past'

To hear all these songs together, please search for 'Jordan Blum's ultimate Jethro Tull playlist' on Spotify.

Jethro Tull albums ranked from best to worst

As always, the top and bottom choices were relatively easy to make, whereas the ones in the middle will fluctuate most for me on any given day. It's no surprise that the band's two album-length songs are my top picks, and the few that follow come naturally since the 1970s was Jethro Tull's top period - if also uneven, as I've placed some in-between records farther down the scale. Likewise, I've always thought that they recaptured that magic in the 1990s, so Roots to Branches, in particular, is a highlight. As for the rest, well, you already know how I feel about that early 1980s production, and while the band did improve later on in the decade, even those aren't too essential to me.

1. *A Passion Play*
2. *Thick as a Brick*
3. *Aqualung*
4. *Songs from the Wood*
5. *Minstrel in the Gallery*
6. *Benefit*
7. *Heavy Horses*
8. *War Child*
9. *Stormwatch*
10. *Roots to Branches*
11. *J-Tull Dot Com*
12. *The Jethro Tull Christmas Album*
13. *Stand Up*
14. *Crest of a Knave*
15. *Rock Island*
16. *A*
17. *Too Old to Rock 'n' Roll, Too Young to Die!*
18. *Catfish Rising*
19. *The Broadsword and the Beast*
20. *This Was*
21. *Under Wraps*

Bibliography

Anderson, Ian. "Surprise – The Abandoned 'War Child' Movie Outline." Jethrotull.com, July 2003,

Bell, Robin. *The History of British Rock and Roll: The Psychedelic Years 1967 – 1969*. Robin Bell, 2017.

Bosso, Joe. "The Real Story Behind Jethro Tull's 'Stand Up'." *Music Aficionado*,

Breznikar, Klemen. "Glenn Cornick Interview about Jethro Tull, Wild Turkey..." *It's Psychedelic Baby Magazine*, Klemen Breznikar, 2011
Espinoza, Barbara. *Driving in Diverse: a Collective Profile of Jethro Tull*. Morris Pub., 1999.

Galipault, Gerry. "TULL'S IAN ANDERSON TAKES HIS MUSIC SERIOUSLY." Chicago Tribune, Chicago Tribune, 12 Oct. 1995.

Glass, Polly. "Opeth Come Clean on What Sorceress Is Really About." *Loudersound*, Future Publishing, 27 Sept. 2016

Grow, Kory. "Jethro Tull's Ian Anderson: My Life in 10 Songs." *Rolling Stone*, Rolling Stone, 27 June 2018

Harr, Douglass. *Rockin' the City of Angels* . Diego Spade Productions, Inc, 2016.

Hotten, Jon. "Every Jethro Tull Album Ranked from Worst to Best." *Loudersound*, Future Publishing, 8 Aug. 2016

Hughes, Rob. "Jethro Tull: Keeping the Folk Fires Burning." *Loudersound*, Future Publishing, 23 Jan. 2015

Hunniford, Gloria. "Ian Anderson embarrasses Gloria Hunniford live on air." *YouTube*, uploaded by Jethrotullforum, 22 June 2011

Masuo, Sandy. "The Jethro Tull Christmas Album." *Rolling Stone*, Rolling Stone, 17 Dec. 2003

Middles, Mick. "In The Mood: The Favourite Albums Of Rush's Geddy Lee ." *The Quietus*, The Quietus , 29 Jan. 2012

Murphy, Sean. "Reappraising Ian Anderson's 'Minstrel in the Gallery'." *PopMatters*, PopMatters, 5 Aug. 2015

Nollen, Scott Allen. *Jethro Tull: a History of the Band, 1968-2001*. McFarland, 2002.

Rabey, Brian. *A Passion Play: the Story of Ian Anderson and Jethro Tull*. Soundcheck, 2013.

Reed, Ryan. "How Jethro Tull Dialed Down Then Rocked Out on 'War Child'." *Ultimate Classic Rock*, Townsquare Media, 14 Oct. 2015.

Reed, Ryan. "How Jethro Tull Ended the '70s With the Underrated 'Stormwatch'." *Ultimate Classic Rock*, Townsquare Media, 14 Sept. 2014,

Rees, Paul. "Let's Party like It's 1399: The Story behind Jethro Tull's Songs From The Wood." *Loudersound*, Future Publishing, 1 Mar. 2017

Romano, Will. *Mountains Come out of the Sky the Illustrated History of Prog Rock*. Backbeat, 2010.

Sleger, Dave. "The Jethro Tull Christmas Album – Jethro Tull | Songs, Reviews, Credits." AllMusic, RhythmOne , 2003.

Voorbij, Jan. "Cup of Wonder, Jethro Tull Lyrics and Annotations." *Cup of Wonder, Jethro Tull Lyrics and Annotations*, Jan Voorbij, 1998.

Wilding, Philip. "Every Jethro Tull Album in Ian Anderson's Own Words." *Loudersound*, Future Publishing Limited, 12 Mar. 2018.

Wilding, Philip. "Ian Anderson: 'Heavy Horses Is a Logical Successor to Songs From The Wood.'" *Loudersound*, Future Publishing, 5 Mar. 2018.

Wilding, Philip. "The Enduring Appeal of Jethro Tull." *Loudersound*, Future Publishing, 5 Mar. 2018.

Wright, Jeb. "Forty Years Of Aqualung: An Interview With Jethro Tull's Martin Barre." *Classic Rock Revisited*, Jeb Wright, 2012.

Would you like to write for Sonicbond Publishing?

At Sonicbond Publishing we are always on the look-out for authors, particularly for our two main series:

On Track. Mixing fact with in depth analysis, the On Track series examines the work of a particular musical artist or group. All genres are considered from easy listening and jazz to 60s soul to 90s pop, via rock and metal.

On Screen. This series looks at the world of film and television. Subjects considered include directors, actors and writers, as well as entire television and film series. As with the On Track series, we balance fact with analysis.

While professional writing experience would, of course, be an advantage the most important qualification is to have real enthusiasm and knowledge of your subject. First-time authors are welcomed, but the ability to write well in English is essential.

Sonicbond Publishing has distribution throughout Europe and North America, and all books are also published in E-book form. Authors will be paid a royalty based on sales of their book.

Further details are available from www.sonicbondpublishing.co.uk. To contact us, complete the contact form there or email info@sonicbondpublishing.co.uk